AN OLD TEST

ANCIENT PATHS

Light and Life from
The Scriptures Jesus Read

TOBY SHOCKEY

RIVERSTONE GROUP
PUBLISHING

DEDICATION

To Hannah,

*The older you become, the more you will understand that the loudest and most frequently heard voices are rarely the ones worth hearing. Ecclesiastes 9:17 says, "The words of the wise heard in quiet are better than the shouting of a ruler among fools." As you are already doing, learn and love the Word of God. Obey it even when it's hard. Seek its quiet wisdom and treasure its words in your heart. Even more importantly, love God supremely. Whatever fleeting things this world has to offer, He is forever – and He is **better.***

Love,
Dad

Ancient Paths – Light and Life from The Scriptures Jesus Read

by Toby Shockey

Copyright © 2020. All rights reserved, including the right to reproduce this book or portions thereof in any form whatsoever. Toby Shockey

For information, contact the author at:
www.tobyshockey.com or www.mountaintime.org

ISBN: 979-8-9857349-5-9

Riverstone Group Publishing

Manufactured in the United States of America

Photo of the author by Nico Zinsmeyer

Unless otherwise noted, all Scripture quotations are from The Holy Bible, English Standard Version. ESV® Text Edition: 2016. Copyright © 2001 by Crossway Bibles, a publishing ministry of Good News Publishers.

CONTENTS

Foreword... 7
Introduction... 9
1. Making the Flat Cakes - 1 Chronicles 9:31 11
2. When We Think We Know - 2 Kings 20:1 13
3. Meaning in Demeaning - 1 Samuel 17:26, 28 15
4. Little by Little - Exodus 23:28-30 17
5. Unintentional Correctness - Job 5:8-9 20
6. Past the Point of Done - 1 Kings 19:9–10 22
7. A Bad Time for Boasting - 1 Kings 20:11 24
8. Logging Your Journey - Exodus 15:22-26 27
9. Shutting Up Shimei - 2 Samuel 16:5-8 29
10. Saved from Yourself - Genesis 37:5–11 31
11. Seasoning - Psalm 1:1-3 33
12. The Fat of the Land - Deuteronomy 31:20-21 35
13. Don't Be Surprised - Psalm 83:1-2 37
14. Walking or Stumbling - Hosea 14:9 39
15. What If It Doesn't Matter? - 2 Kings 22:1-2 41
16. Ways and Means - 2 Chronicles 27:6 44
17. Just Keep Showing Up - Jeremiah 48:21-26 46
18. All of the Above - Jeremiah 20:12-15 48
19. Here Today, Gone Tomorrow - Ecclesiastes 3:16-22 50
20. A "Briefs" Object Lesson - Jeremiah 13:1-4, 11 52
21. The Pursuit of Nothing - Ecclesiastes 1:1-18 54
22. Today Is the Day - Psalm 118:24 57
23. Barren, Broken and Blessed - 1 Samuel 1:1-2 60

24. The Curse of an Easy Road - 1 Kings 11:1-6 62
25. Work, Work, Work - Ecclesiastes 2:18-26 65
26. Follow the Pillar - Exodus 13:17-18, 21-22 67
27. When the King Is Dead - Isaiah 6:1-3 69
28. The Boring Hero - Judges 3:7-11 71
29. Using What Is Left - Judges 3:15-17, 21-22 73
30. When the Glory Isn't Yours - Judges 4:4-9 75
31. Not How But Who - Judges 4-5 77
32. But We Didn't Ask for That - Judges 6:1-10 79
33. The Hiding Warrior - Judges 6:11-16 81
34. First Things First - Judges 6:24-27 83
35. Faith or Fleece? - Judges 6:36-40 85
36. Less Is More - Judges 7:2-7 87
37. Making It About Me - Judges 7:16-18 89
38. Weapons of War - Judges 7:19-22 91
39. Time and Time Again - Ecclesiastes 3:1-8 93
40. Hosea: Costly Forgiveness - Hosea 3:1-5 95
41. Joel: The Restoration Project - Joel 2:23-27 97
42. Amos: Worthless Worship - Amos 5:21-24 99
43. Obadiah: God Noticed - Obadiah 2-4, 15 101
44. Jonah: Chased by Grace - Jonah 2:1-9 103
45. Micah: Who Is Like Yahweh? - Micah 7:18-20 105
46. Nahum: When God Throws Filth - Nahum 3:5-7 107
47. Habakkuk: Asking God Why - Habakkuk 1:2-4 109
48. Zephaniah: The Day of the Lord - Zephaniah 1:12-14 112
49. Haggai: Putting Me First - Haggai 1:2-6 114
50. Zechariah: When the Enemy Accuses - Zechariah 3:1-5 116
51. Malachi: Don't Bring Leftovers - Malachi 1:11-14 118

FOREWORD

Ugh! Who reads the Old Testament? Those people are so old they did not even have the internet. How could they get anything done or have any fun? I mean – they could not even stream reruns of "The Flintstones." Now that's old.

I understand why some may think of the Old Testament as outdated. However, I like to think of the characters and stories that are shared in the pages of the Old Testament more like superheroes. Think about it – superheroes are good at something but also have a fatal flaw. They are for the people and do their best to eradicate evil and wrongdoing. That is exciting!

In reality, the characters and their stories that are shared in the Old Testament are much like ours. They are regular, ordinary people going about their daily lives and "Bam!" – God interrupts the mundane. I feel pretty confident that many of you who have picked up this book are regular, ordinary people going about your daily lives and "Bam!" – God has interrupted your mundane life. How exciting is that?

Think about that for a second. God knows you well enough that he has reached out to you to join His team. You. You? You! A regular, ordinary person who goes to work every day, cooks dinner, cleans toilets and argues with your kids over cleaning up their room. Yeah, that you.

Well, my great friend, Toby, is an ordinary person whose mundane life was interrupted by God. Toby is a student of God's Word and has always had an affinity for the Old Testament stories. Throughout his writings, you are able to see how these characters and their stories apply to life - your life and, more importantly, how they relate to your faith-life and journey.

With every devotion you read in this book, you are reading more than superhero stories. You are reading people's life stories and their interactions with God and His people. To me, the amazing things about reading these stories is these people are the same people who are in the Hall of Faith that Hebrews 11 tells us about. Yeah. These same people are now cheering you on in your race of faith. They know how difficult, but possible, it is to know and follow God.

The race of life is a marathon combined with a triathlon combined with a decathlon. In other words, it is a long, winding road with multiple obstacles and opportunities. Take some time and work your way through these stories and learn from those that have gone before you - where there is danger or where there is opportunity.

As you read and contemplate the stories in the following pages, you'll get to know people who have encouraged and challenged Toby's faith and life. If it helps, imagine an old guy with a coffee cup and some flat cakes sitting across from you, telling you stories from the "good ol' days" . . . sit, listen and learn from those who have gone before us.

–Dr. Chris Little
Lead Pastor, Crosspoint Community Church
Adjunct Instructor, Colorado Christian University

INTRODUCTION

Devotions from the Old Testament – seriously? Yes, but at least some humor is mixed into them. Not long ago, I preached a series on the book of Habakkuk entitled "Habakkuk: O Lord, Why?" and suggested that "O Lord, why?" was probably also the reaction of most people when they found out the preaching series was on the book of Habakkuk. Well, you might have the very same question for this book, but I am thankful that you're giving it a chance.

Truth be told, some of the devotions in this book are not just from the Old Testament but are even from obscure, unexpected places in the Old Testament. Some of the passages will be familiar to you, but it's likely that many of them will not be. And that's by design. The Bible includes chapters and sections and even books that many of us rarely see, but hopefully a devotion from an obscure place in Scripture will whet the appetite.

But if you are still asking why the Old Testament, that's a good question. After all, we are talking about the Old Testament. We might think of several reasons, but the main reason is that the Old Testament points to Jesus and is only understood in the light of Jesus. Not only is Jesus predicted and promised, but the story of God's people reveals their desperate need for a Savior…and ours! Related to that, the Old Testament is as much the Word of God as the New Testament. The Bible that Jesus and all the New Testament writers read was the Old Testament. Our understanding of the New Testament is deeper and richer through the study of the Old.

Finally, when Paul wrote to Timothy, he said, "All Scripture is breathed out by God and profitable for teaching, for reproof, for correction, and for training in righteousness, that the man of God may be complete, equipped for every good work" (2 Timothy 3:16-17). The writer of

Hebrews added, "For the word of God is living and active, sharper than any two-edged sword, piercing to the division of soul and of spirit, of joints and of marrow, and discerning the thoughts and intentions of the heart" (Hebrews 4:12). With those descriptions in mind, let's remember that the New Testament was still being written at the time. While we know these descriptions are true of the New Testament, they were primarily written about the Old. We read and study the Old Testament because it is powerful, relevant and life changing.

Yahweh spoke these words through Jeremiah the prophet:

> Thus says the LORD:
> "Stand by the roads, and look,
> and ask for the *ancient paths,* (emphasis added)
> where the good way is; and walk in it,
> and find rest for your souls" (Jeremiah 6:16).

Look for the ancient paths and walk in them. Look for the good way and take it. As you do, you will find rest for your souls. But then, ominously, He adds, "But they said, 'We will not walk in it.'"

As you read through these relatively short passages of Scripture, you will be walking on the ancient paths and the good way. God willing, the devotional comments and reflection questions will help and not hinder your meditation upon and response to the Word. May the Holy Spirit enable you to find instruction for your mind, encouragement for your heart and rest for your soul.

–Toby Shockey
www.mountaintime.org
www.tobyshockey.com

DAY 1

MAKING THE FLAT CAKES

*...and Mattithiah, one of the Levites,
the firstborn of Shallum the Korahite,
was entrusted with making the flat cakes.*

1 Chronicles 9:31

We don't know a lot about Mattithiah, but what we do know is this: *he made the flat cakes.* If there were any thick cakes to be made, someone else made them because Mattithiah made the flat cakes. You may remember the old commercial with the guy who gets up early every morning chanting, "Gotta make the doughnuts." It may have been much like that for Mattithiah since making the flat cakes doesn't sound like the most exciting or glamorous job.

When we read about this today, we don't attribute much significance to it. In fact, it may not have even been regarded as an important role – even in Mattithiah's day. Although making the flat cakes was probably not the most glamorous task, we need to keep some things in mind. First, making the flat cakes was a part of the worship practice in the temple in the Old Testament. Serving the Lord in any capacity is significant. Also, let's not overlook the fact that Mattithiah making the flat cakes is mentioned in the Bible. Evidently, this service was significant enough to God for it to be mentioned in Scripture. "Mr. Flat Cakes" may have never had a huge following or received a lot of fanfare; but the task of making the flat cakes was *entrusted* to him, and evidently he was faithful to this calling.

How frightening to think that so many of us are either ineffective or inactive in our service to God because we are more interested in the praise of people. We often aren't willing to faithfully "make the flat cakes" because no applause or recognition will result from all our efforts. We're looking for a much more glamorous and attention-getting way of serving God where we can get the glory and recognition that we think we deserve. But God sees what is done in secret and rewards faithfulness in the small things. Service that might seem insignificant and unworthy of notice has God's full attention. The significance of a task is not in how much applause we receive for doing it but in the worthiness of the One we are serving.

HEAD TO HEART

- Why do we attribute more value or significance to certain tasks – even in the service of the Lord and His people?

- Are you truly willing to serve the Lord with a joyful heart – even when you probably will not receive appreciation?

- In what specific ways is God calling you to "make the flat cakes"?

DAY 2

WHEN WE THINK WE KNOW

In those days Hezekiah became sick and was at the point of death. And Isaiah the prophet the son of Amoz came to him and said to him, "Thus says the LORD, 'Set your house in order, for you shall die; you shall not recover.' Then Hezekiah turned his face to the wall and prayed to the LORD, saying, "Now, O LORD, please remember how I have walked before you in faithfulness and with a whole heart, and have done what is good in your sight." And Hezekiah wept bitterly. And before Isaiah had gone out of the middle court, the word of the LORD came to him: "Turn back, and say to Hezekiah the leader of my people, Thus says the LORD, the God of David your father: I have heard your prayer; I have seen your tears. Behold, I will heal you. On the third day you shall go up to the house of the LORD, and I will add fifteen years to your life. I will deliver you and this city out of the hand of the king of Assyria, and I will defend this city for my own sake and for my servant David's sake."

2 Kings 20:1-6

Hezekiah had been a strong and godly leader in Judah for many years when the Lord spoke to him through Isaiah. The word from the prophet was crushing; and Hezekiah prayed, "Now, O LORD, please remember how I have walked before you in faithfulness and with a whole heart, and have done what is good in your sight." Hezekiah was arguing that he deserved much better treatment after all he had done for the Lord. Before we are too critical of Hezekiah's response, we might remember that he would not have had the understanding of Heaven that we do and that he did not have his own example by which to learn as we do.

But perhaps surprisingly, in response to Hezekiah's prayer, God agreed to heal him and granted him 15 more years to live. While we don't fully know what drove Hezekiah to pray this way and to be so reluctant to reach the end of his life, he must have been grateful to know he had more time and how long that span of time would be. But Hezekiah's life is a great example that we clearly don't know what God knows. We think we know what is best and what the best outcome would be, but we are mistaken.

Now, of course, God's sovereignty is still in effect over this whole story; but what we see is that truly nothing good happened in the 15 extra years Hezekiah was given. First, he acted foolishly in showing the king of Babylon the treasures of Judah. There was no good reason to do that. His actions may not have been evil, but it was a foolish thing to do. (2 Kings 20:12-19); but the worst was yet to come.

In the next chapter, we learn that Manasseh, the son of Hezekiah, became king when he was 12 years old. (2 Kings 21:1) We later learn that he was perhaps the most wicked king Judah had ever known. Manasseh essentially reversed all of the good that Hezekiah had done; but if Hezekiah had not lived those extra 15 years, Manasseh would have never been born. Again, God obviously could have prevented all that from happening; but there we see that we are like Hezekiah. We just know what God should do and tell him so. If God is doing something or not doing something that doesn't make sense to us, we do well to pause and remember that we're the ones with limited understanding.

HEAD TO HEART

- Have you ever (or often!) felt that you deserved better than what you seemed to be getting from God?

- How would you respond if it were revealed to you that your days were numbered? (Keep in mind – they are!)

- Knowing that God could have certainly prevented all the evil that Manasseh would do, how do you respond when God does things beyond your understanding?

DAY 3

MEANING IN DEMEANING

And David said to the men who stood by him, "What shall be done for the man who kills this Philistine and takes away the reproach from Israel? For who is this uncircumcised Philistine, that he should defy the armies of the living God?" ... Now Eliab his eldest brother heard when he spoke to the men. And Eliab's anger was kindled against David, and he said, "Why have you come down? And with whom have you left those few sheep in the wilderness? I know your presumption and the evil of your heart, for you have come down to see the battle."

1 Samuel 17:26, 28

If anyone has ever eaten their words, David's older brother Eliab experienced a smorgasbord. But even if they aren't all blood relatives, Eliab has an untold number of descendants. David simply had followed his father's instructions, leaving his flock in someone's else care to bring provisions to his brothers at the scene of the battle. When David arrived, he heard the Philistine giant Goliath call for a challenger among the ranks of Israel. David came to the battle with no agenda but was astounded to discover that Goliath had defied not only Israel but the Living God.

Eliab, who himself obviously was afraid to face Goliath, laid into David. Eliab belittled David and questioned his motives for even being there. Notice what he asked David: "... with whom have you left those *few sheep*. . . ?" In other words, "Why have you left your small, insignificant role and place in life to come here?" This was followed by Eliab accusing David of evil motives. Clearly, Eliab either had difficulty expressing his affection for his little brother; or he really had it in for David! The fact is that Eliab despised David for the same reason that King Saul would

– pure and simple jealousy. When the prophet Samuel came to anoint the next king of Israel, he passed over all the sons of Jesse, beginning with Eliab, and finally anointed David as the king – once David finally arrived from tending his few sheep! (1 Samuel 16:6-13)

Without much thought, you probably can identify who has been the Eliab in your life. For whatever reason, they dismissed, demeaned and disregarded you. They questioned your motives and accused your heart. But just like Eliab, they were wrong. That person saw you the way they did; but thankfully, that isn't at all what God sees. We would be less than honest to say that there wasn't at least a small measure of *"nyah-nyah"* in our hearts when our accusers are proven wrong, but hopefully our stance is more gratitude to God than vindication of ourselves.

Unfortunately, we might see ourselves as David in this story and never consider our ability to demean others. Sometimes after being the target of an Eliab, we become Eliab to someone else and our jealous, self-promoting motives are revealed. We easily can be condescending and dismissive because we assume that we know what God can and cannot do in a person's life. When God does great things in a person's life, we can hope we were among those who gave encouragement. As easy as it is to think of the Eliabs in our lives, hopefully we can more easily remember those who have encouraged us along the way.

And by the way, Eliab, your little brother David did not come to watch the battle – he came to *win* it.

HEAD TO HEART
- Who has been the Eliab in your life? Is the attitude of your heart towards them grace and forgiveness?

- When you have treated other people poorly, what do you think was driving that and made it seem acceptable at the time?

- What kept a young David from being destroyed by criticism? How do you lay hold of that same ability for yourself?

DAY 4

LITTLE BY LITTLE

And I will send hornets before you, which shall drive out the Hivites, the Canaanites, and the Hittites from before you. I will not drive them out from before you in one year, lest the land become desolate and the wild beasts multiply against you. Little by little I will drive them out from before you, until you have increased and possess the land.

Exodus 23:28-30

God knew exactly what He was doing. The land He had promised to the Israelites was theirs for the taking, and victory was assured. All that was required of them was to fight one battle at a time. Rather than drive out the current occupants of the land all at once, the Lord had an even better plan. If the land were to lie dormant until the time that the Israelites were able to occupy every acre, it would have become desolate and the wild beasts too numerous. Instead God chose to allow the inhabitants to stay and continue to work the land until the time that His people were ready to drive them away. According to the plan, the land would be ready for them once they were ready to take it. The conquest would be little by little, but victory was certain. And there was much more at stake than just land.

Sadly, Israel succeeded in snatching defeat from the jaws of victory. Although the land – with all its abundance – was theirs for the taking, in large measure, they failed to take what was theirs. As a result, God's people would be tormented continually by those whom they should have driven out. (Judges 1-2) Fear, foolish alliances and apathy all led to their failure. All at once, God could have made a parking lot of the land for them so that they simply could move in unhindered; but He had a better plan that was for their good. "Little by little" would have been a huge success - if only they had followed the plan.

The people of Israel wanted a smooth, easy and immediate transition from the Exodus to the Promised Land; but this would have been disastrous. If the rest of their history is any indication, they would have turned away from the Lord about 12 minutes after entering the land. Having received what was promised, in their immaturity, what further use would they have for God? They never would have learned of His faithfulness and His provision and their continual need for His presence if there had been no battles to fight or trials to endure in the process of taking possession.

In a shocking development, we have so much in common with the Israelites. In the story of their colossal failure, God holds up a mirror for us. Just like the people of Israel, we love the idea of victory and conquest over our enemies but often fail to engage in the battle that is necessary for the victory. We miss out because often we won't do the things that are necessary to experience what God has for us.

For us, the opportunity may not be a Promised Land; but God may well be wanting to give to us a blessing but will not do so apart from our persistent participation in the process. Worse than never having our "land" is possessing the land without having learned the things that God wanted to teach us in the process. All too often, we just want the land and become impatient with the monotonous, slow pace of getting there. The Lord wants us to receive the blessing but only after we have been made ready. As with the people of Israel, the war is waged one battle at a time; but the outcome is sure if we will move at His direction and at His pace.

HEAD TO HEART

- How do you respond when God doesn't seem to be moving at your pace?

- We can often see the wisdom of God in how He deals with His people in the Bible, but why is it more difficult to recognize that same wisdom as He deals with us?

- What are the promises that you are trusting God to fulfill in His timing and His way?

DAY 5

UNINTENTIONAL CORRECTNESS

As for me, I would seek God, and to God would I commit my cause, who does great things and unsearchable, marvelous things without number.

Job 5:8-9

Sometimes people can be absolutely right without even knowing what they're talking about. They aren't even right in the sense that they intended to be; but somehow, they're still right. We might call that "unintentional correctness." Job's friend Eliphaz may very well be the author of unintentional correctness (but he didn't mean to be).

We remember, from the opening chapters of Job, that the devil asked God for permission to afflict Job; and God granted him that permission and even set limits on what he could and could not do to Job. This celestial conversation launched a series of tragedies and disasters in Job's life that brought Job way beyond the end of himself. *Yet every tragedy was allowed by God.*

As Job understandably laments his situation and his inability to understand it, Eliphaz and friends enter the story and begin to spew their vast wisdom all over Job. Perhaps one of the reasons God allows difficulty and suffering in our lives is so that we don't sound like Eliphaz when we're trying to encourage and minister to someone who is hurting. As Job writhed in his suffering, Eliphaz was there to point out, "As for me, I would seek God, and to God would I commit my cause."

Suddenly astonished at the breadth and depth of such profound spiritual insight, Job probably wished he'd thought of that! "So I should seek God? Well, I suppose I could give praying a shot." What Eliphaz simply could not fathom was that Job *had* sought God and *had* committed his way to the Lord that made him the target of both the devil's attacks and the Lord's testing. To Eliphaz, God only *delivered* people from suffering – He could not allow suffering or be the cause of it. The pop theology of Eliphaz is alive and well today; and we can point to certain preachers on TV, wearing expensive suits, to prove it.

Eliphaz was accidentally right in saying that God does great and unsearchable things, but he didn't see that God was doing some of those very things at that moment in Job's life. In new ways, Job undoubtedly was marveling at the ways of God although "marvelous" might not have been his choice of words at the time. If you've been walking with the Lord for very long, you've probably done some of your own marveling at God's ways and works in your life and perhaps have found them to be as great and unsearchable as Job did. Like Job, you may have discovered that trials came *because* you sought the Lord and committed your way to Him - not because you hadn't.

Many have bought into the convenient lie that God's ultimate goal is for us to be comfortable. When our circumstances aren't all that comfortable, we find that Eliphaz and his friends are still around – always at the ready with slogans, cliches and encouraging half-truths. The trying circumstances of our lives reveal that God is actively at work in us; and for those things, we can be grateful. Just don't expect the Eliphazes in your life to understand (unless it's unintentional).

HEAD TO HEART
- What are some of the dangers in giving unsolicited counsel or advice? In what ways have you been the recipient?

- How do God's dealings with Job contradict the "prosperity gospel" that is prevalent today?

- Are you blaming the enemy (or an enemy) for the things that God is allowing in your life to help you grow?

DAY 6

PAST THE POINT OF DONE

There he came to a cave and lodged in it. And behold, the word of the LORD came to him, and he said to him, "What are you doing here, Elijah?" He said, "I have been very jealous for the LORD, the God of hosts. For the people of Israel have forsaken your covenant, thrown down your altars, and killed your prophets with the sword, and I, even I only, am left, and they seek my life, to take it away."

1 Kings 19:9-10

Hiding away in a cave was not the highlight of Elijah's life or ministry, but a long series of events had brought him to a place he neither expected nor wanted to be. Before this, there had been years of tedious preparation in the wilderness during days of famine. He had been fed by the ravens and learned to depend on the Lord for everything – especially when his water source ran dry. (1 Kings 17) Then there was a huge victory over the prophets of Baal and Asherah where Elijah called down fire from heaven in the presence of all the people of Israel. But after the big showdown at Mount Carmel was over and on the heels of victory, Elijah suddenly had to flee for his life. (1 Kings 18) By the time he reached the cave, Elijah was *done*. Exhausted and dejected, he didn't lack for self-pity either, but such is life in the cave.

The time in the cave was a rough experience for Elijah, but the isolation gave him a chance to rest and recover. More importantly, Elijah now had the opportunity to vomit the multitude of his frustrations and the perceived unfairness of his lot in life. And God showed that He was able to handle every complaint. Besides, God already knew these terrible moments were coming – even in the glorious times when Elijah was calling down fire from heaven and slaughtering the prophets of

Baal. Elijah may have thought he was done, but God wasn't done with him. For all that the cave experience did to Elijah, God's plans hadn't changed. And after the cave experience, there was still more for Elijah to do.

Maybe you've been in the cave like Elijah. Or maybe you're spelunking along in your own cave right now. The experience may not be a literal cave, but it is every bit as real and you are every bit as done as Elijah. You gave it your best; you tried your hardest and thought you were doing what God said to do; but things didn't work out as you'd hoped.

When that happens, all of our ambitions, determination and best intentions don't really matter because we are simply done. At least, we believe we are. But neither Elijah's "declaration of done" nor ours changes God's plan or God's purpose. In fact, the place where we are done is often where God begins and getting us there was His doing also. He isn't surprised by what has or hasn't happened to us nor is He frantically trying to figure out what to do now. The cave is merely preparation for what God is going to do next. Our being done is only the beginning. He may have brought us to the cave; but when He's ready, He'll bring us out of it, too.

HEAD TO HEART
- In what times of your life were you like Elijah and just *done*?
- How does God gently speaking to Elijah in his frustration encourage or admonish you?
- How might God be using what is happening in your life now to prepare you for something later?

DAY 7

A BAD TIME FOR BOASTING

*And the king of Israel answered,
"Tell him, 'Let not him who straps on his
armor boast himself as he who takes it off.'"*

1 Kings 20:11

King Ahab said very little that was worth repeating; but as the saying goes, even a blind hog can find an acorn occasionally. At least this time, Ahab was right – the time for boasting isn't while you're still preparing for battle. Ahab had every reason to be afraid of Ben-Hadad, the king of Syria who was continually threatening him. Yet Ahab responded not with a threat but with a proverb. Events would reveal the truth of the proverb as Ben-Hadad's boasting proved to be premature. Even though Ahab wasn't exactly the best or wisest king Israel would ever have, the Bible gives us a profound truth out of his mouth: "Let not him who straps on his armor boast himself as he who takes it off."

So what does that *mean*? Besides the fact that boasting isn't a great idea at any point, the proverb speaks about experience. If you haven't gone through the battle, then it's a bad idea to talk as one who has. And that's where this little proverb can get annoyingly convicting. We are all too often quick to assume that we know much more than we do, especially when it comes to situations involving others. We often struggle in knowing what to do when difficult situations arise in our lives, but we assume to know exactly what someone else should do in their situation. If we wrestle with discerning God's will for our lives, how is it that we "just know" what God wants someone else to do? Maybe that's a little presumptuous.

When Job went through his ordeal, he had friends who thought they knew exactly what God was saying and doing. After going through what he did, Job understandably had a few questions for God. Sadly, Job's friends were there with all of the answers. Job's friends lacked the humility to recognize they were not in his shoes and had never been through what he was experiencing. But somehow they just knew precisely why this was happening and exactly what Job should do. Know anyone like that?

The sad thing is that Job's friends started out right. The Bible says that when Job's friends first arrived after all of the calamities, they didn't even recognize Job and wept for him. "And they sat with him on the ground seven days and seven nights, and no one spoke a word to him, for they saw that his suffering was very great" (Job 2:13). We can learn so much from that. Sadly, after the seven days had passed, Job's friends started talking, and they didn't stop until about 35 chapters later. Throughout their platitudes, Job's friends boasted as those who had gone through the same battle that Job did and were somehow qualified to instruct him even though they couldn't begin to fathom what Job had experienced.

All too often, we are guilty of seeing a situation in someone else's life and spouting something to the effect that "If they would just...." The fact that we don't know everything about their situation and that we're not in their shoes doesn't prevent us from having a strong and set opinion about what they should do.

Sure, speaking truth into someone else's life can be a blessing for the speaker and the hearer. Many times, we're just in too big of a hurry to speak. For good reason, the Bible tells us to be quick to hear but *slow* to speak. Maybe Proverbs 18:2 says it best, "A fool takes no pleasure in understanding, but only in expressing his opinion." We do well not to offer the vastness of our wisdom and knowledge to others unless and until they have asked us for it (and sometimes not even then!) Genuinely listening first will usually keep us from speaking presumptuously and foolishly.

What about those who really have been through the battle? It's true that those who are putting on their armor shouldn't boast as those who take it off, but those who have actually been through battles typically aren't boasting about it. If you've really been through a battle, you know that God's grace and strength alone brought you through that battle. You don't boast about it because no boasting is needed. Surviving the battle wasn't about you but Him. If you've been through a battle, you also know that the time to shed the armor is not just yet. We can expect that another battle is coming. May the truth and wisdom of God's Word empower us to fight our *own* battles and fight them well.

HEAD TO HEART

- What are the biggest battles you have fought in your life? How have these experiences equipped you to encourage others?

- Do you find it easier to know what someone else should do in their situation than it is to know the best course of action for yourself?

- How does God's grace disqualify any of us from boasting?

DAY 8

LOGGING YOUR JOURNEY

Then Moses made Israel set out from the Red Sea, and they went into the wilderness of Shur. They went three days in the wilderness and found no water. When they came to Marah, they could not drink the water of Marah because it was bitter; therefore it was named Marah. And the people grumbled against Moses, saying, "What shall we drink?" And he cried to the LORD, and the LORD showed him a log, and he threw it into the water, and the water became sweet. There the LORD made for them a statute and a rule, and there he tested them, saying, "If you will diligently listen to the voice of the LORD your God, and do that which is right in his eyes, and give ear to his commandments and keep all his statutes, I will put none of the diseases on you that I put on the Egyptians, for I am the LORD, your healer."

Exodus 15:22-26

How many days does it take to get from Glory to Grumble? For the people of Israel, the journey was just three days of walking. Having just been delivered from Egyptian slavery and rescued from Pharaoh's army by the miraculous crossing of the Red Sea, the people quickly griped about the lack of water. When they finally found water after three days in the wilderness, the water they found was bitter. But there was more bitter than just the water.

The people grumbled, and Moses prayed and threw a log in the bitter water. God made the water sweet, but that wasn't all that God did that day. The Lord also revealed His nature and His character to a people that would continue to demonstrate that they really didn't know their God. The name by which He revealed Himself at this time was Yahweh-Rophe, the Lord our Healer.

Now the Lord has been known to work in mysterious ways, but it does seem a little strange that He presented Himself by that particular name when there was no mention of disease or sickness. In fact, the context in which the Scriptures introduce the Lord as our Healer is not a context of sickness and disease but of *bitterness*. The water may have been bitter at first, but the bitterness must have run deep in the people as well. Hundreds of years of slavery will do that. So it wasn't a coincidence that this was the context for the Lord to declare "I am the LORD, your healer."

Bitterness is easy to perceive. Being around a bitter person is a lot like tasting something that's bitter. Realized or not, that bitterness affects everything around it. People will call on Yahweh-Rophe to heal their diseases but never consider a long-harbored bitterness may have ultimately led to that sickness. That might sound like a stretch, but it's a bad idea to underestimate the harm that years of festering resentment and grumbling can bring.

Just like the people of Israel, the Lord brings us through different seasons in our lives, and often we need a measure of healing from one season before we're ready to move to the next. We don't have to look hard to find sources of resentment. They have a way of finding us. But God brings healing because He is the Healer, and He has a long history of turning bitter into sweet.

HEAD TO HEART

- Why do you think God didn't bring the people to a place with water right away? Why would He bring them to bitter water after they already had waited for several days?

- Would the people who are close to you describe you as a bitter person? Are there areas of your life that need healing from bitterness?

- How can you best handle being around a person who seems to be very bitter?

DAY 9

SHUTTING UP SHIMEI

When King David came to Bahurim, there came out a man of the family of the house of Saul, whose name was Shimei, the son of Gera, and as he came he cursed continually. And he threw stones at David and at all the servants of King David .... And Shimei said as he cursed, "Get out, get out, you man of blood, you worthless man! The LORD has avenged on you all the blood of the house of Saul, in whose place you have reigned, and the LORD has given the kingdom into the hand of your son Absalom. See, your evil is on you, for you are a man of blood."

2 Samuel 16:5-8

David already wasn't having a good day. Any day that a king is forced to flee his kingdom because his own son has seized power is a really bad day, but even a really bad day can get worse. As King David fled from his son Absalom, Shimei arrived on the scene and launched a barrage of accusations that added insult to injury. Don't bad things seem to always be accompanied by *more* bad things?

Have you ever noticed that often the ones who hurl the loudest accusations are also dead wrong? The passing of time eventually proves it. The most vicious and boisterous accusations usually are launched only from a safe distance. Shimei threw rocks and curses only because a canyon separated him from David and his army. Also, there is no such thing as good timing for vicious accusations. What could have been said at any time, in fact, was said on a really bad day for David. Shimei saw an opportunity and used it to kick David when he already was down.

We shouldn't be overly surprised that all of this happened to David because we too have probably been on the receiving end of some rocks and curses. David's response to Shimei (and ultimately the Lord) is instructive if we will heed its wisdom and humility. The easiest thing to do in a situation like that is to respond in kind. An immediate offer came from one of David's men to take Shimei's head off, which reflects our typical response to this kind of thing.

David would not allow it and said, "... Leave him alone, and let him curse, for the LORD has told him to. It may be that the LORD will look on the wrong done to me, and that the LORD will repay me with good for his cursing today" (2 Samuel 16:11-12). For David, it certainly wasn't the first time he had been falsely accused. Yes, the day would come when Shimei would get what he had coming but not on this day and not by David's hand. (1 Kings 2:36-46)

When malicious accusations are hurled our way, we face the same choice that David did and hopefully will act as wisely. First, we do well to consider if even a shred of truth can be found in the accusation – even if most of it is patently false. Can we learn from anything – even if the words are hurtful? Truly, some of David's misery on that day was self-inflicted. Is there any chance that part of ours may be also?

On other occasions, the accusations that come against us are thoroughly and utterly false. At that point, we can expend enormous amounts of time and energy seeking to defend our good name and reputation, or we can entrust ourselves to the Lord who knows. In either scenario, the wise response is characterized by humility and the recognition that ultimately only one opinion matters. Long before Shimei came crawling back to apologize, the Lord had granted victory to David because he let God be his Defender.

HEAD TO HEART

- If you have ever been falsely accused, how did you handle it?

- Why is it so difficult to let God handle those who bring accusations against us instead of taking matters into our own hands?

- Have you ever been more like Shimei in the story? What can or what did you do to make it right?

DAY 10

SAVED FROM YOURSELF

Now Joseph had a dream, and when he told it to his brothers they hated him even more. He said to them, "Hear this dream that I have dreamed: Behold, we were binding sheaves in the field, and behold, my sheaf arose and stood upright. And behold, your sheaves gathered around it and bowed down to my sheaf." His brothers said to him, "Are you indeed to reign over us? Or are you indeed to rule over us?" So they hated him even more for his dreams and for his words. Then he dreamed another dream and told it to his brothers and said, "Behold, I have dreamed another dream. Behold, the sun, the moon, and eleven stars were bowing down to me." But when he told it to his father and to his brothers, his father rebuked him and said to him, "What is this dream that you have dreamed? Shall I and your mother and your brothers indeed come to bow ourselves to the ground before you?" And his brothers were jealous of him, but his father kept the saying in mind.

Genesis 37:5-11

What would have happened to Joseph if he had never been sold into slavery by his brothers? Since we know how the story of Joseph turns out in the end, we might not have considered that before. Of course, God's plan included Joseph ending up in Egypt. And God already was orchestrating events to save Abraham's offspring from starvation and to set in motion the factors that many years later would lead to the Exodus. But what about Joseph himself?

There can be no doubt that God gave Joseph these dreams about his brothers bowing down to him. Perhaps Joseph held onto the dreams, and they later helped him hold on to the belief that God was preparing something great for him – even as he sat in an Egyptian jail year after year, simply waiting. But none of that suggests he should have shared those dreams with his brothers. That was a big mistake. How did he expect them to react? What man would be thrilled to be told that he someday would bow down to his little brother?

They all knew Joseph was the favorite son – even Joseph. But what if the trials of Joseph's life never happened? Joseph likely would have turned out to be an intolerable, entitled brat that no one could stand to be around. *Before God used Joseph to save his brothers from starving, God used impossible circumstances to save Joseph from himself.* If you don't understand why God has you where He does right now, the Lord very well may be in the process of rescuing you from something you don't even know about. That something may even be you!

HEAD TO HEART

- If revealing the dreams to his family was the wrong thing to do, how could Joseph have better handled the situation?

- When you sense the Holy Spirit speaking to you, how do you determine if it is or is not appropriate to share this information with others?

- How has God's discipline and correction saved you from yourself?

DAY 11

SEASONING

Blessed is the man who walks not in the counsel of the wicked, nor stands in the way of sinners, nor sits in the seat of scoffers; but his delight is in the law of the LORD, and on his law he meditates day and night. He is like a tree planted by streams of water that yields its fruit in its season, and its leaf does not wither. In all that he does, he prospers.

Psalm 1:1-3

God had a good idea when He created seasons. The monotony of a long, hot summer would be unbearable if fall weren't going to follow it. Many probably would tire of winter if spring weren't going to come eventually. We need variety in our lives but not just as it relates to the weather. God walks us through various seasons in our lives – some glorious, some difficult and, in most cases, both. Psalm 1:3 speaks about the one who trusts in the Lord: "He is like a tree planted by streams of water that yields its fruit in its season, and its leaf does not wither. In all that he does, he prospers."

We would love to think that each season of our lives is going to be fruitful; but the picture in this verse is that seasons of preparation, growing and pruning come before the seasons of bearing fruit. The tree always is connected to and receiving from the streams of water, so its leaf does not wither. Only at certain times, though, is it bearing fruit. Only at the appointed time is there a harvest.

As you read this, you likely can relate. It may seem like the season of life in which you find yourself is anything but fruitful. Likely that is because you aren't seeing much of a harvest – right now. Instead you are in a season of preparation for the season to which God will bring you. Pruning and growing take place here; and yes, there may be quite a bit of "fertilizer" that we must walk through in the season of preparation as well. But all that preparation is purposed and essential for what God is going to do. What an opportunity to trust Him, to sink our roots in deeper and see each circumstance as part of God's design. We generally grow the most when the "fertilizer" abounds in our circumstances. As surely as God causes the seasons to change, so He will bring newness and fruitfulness in its season.

HEAD TO HEART

- What words would describe your current season of life?

- If you are in a season of preparation, how will you seek to grow in it?

- If you are in a season of abundance, how did God prepare you for the things He is doing now?

DAY 12

THE FAT OF THE LAND

For when I have brought them into the land flowing with milk and honey, which I swore to give to their fathers, and they have eaten and are full and grown fat, they will turn to other gods and serve them, and despise me and break my covenant. . . . For I know what they are inclined to do even today, before I have brought them into the land that I swore to give.

Deuteronomy 31:20-21

Moses wasn't overly optimistic about what would happen when the people of Israel entered the Promised Land. Then again, the track record they had established in the previous 40 years didn't offer a lot of reasons to have high expectations. From bitter complaining to episodes of idolatry to a generation's fearful refusal to enter the land, the Israelites had not set the bar very high. Although Moses would be out of the picture, he anticipated that they would continue to fail after finally entering the land.

Notice the progression of what would happen. Upon entering the land, the people would eat and become full, but they would not be satisfied. After growing full, they would continue to eat and become fat. The excess would cause them to turn away and eventually despise the Lord. They would have what they wanted and have it in abundance, and that same abundance would end up being the reason they would turn away from the Lord. Now that they wouldn't be wandering and waiting in the wilderness, what was the need for God?

As for you, you've likely noticed that you don't have everything you'd like to have. You have prayed for God to do certain things, and God has answered your prayer – by saying *no*. We are slow to admit that the things we want could be the things that end up making us turn away from the Lord once we have them. As the people of Israel would prove, we not only need a Savior, but we must be denied certain things to be *reminded* that we need a Savior.

God has said no to us for good reason or at least required us to wait until what we are requesting will be a blessing instead of a curse. He is merciful to deny us the things that will cause us to turn away from Him, and we are wise to surrender to His mercy when His answer is no.

HEAD TO HEART

- Why would God bring them into the land, knowing its abundance would lead to their idolatry?

- For what have you asked God and received an answer of no (or wait)?

- Can you trust God in the times He says "yes" and in the times He says "no"?

DAY 13

DON'T BE SURPRISED

O God, do not keep silence;
do not hold your peace or be still, O God! For behold,
your enemies make an uproar;
those who hate you have raised their heads.

Psalm 83:1-2

If we are even remotely aware of what is happening around us, we see the sad reality that some people – at least ostensibly – hate God. While it may be difficult for us to relate to that or even understand the heart of a God-hater, this condition is nothing new. Ours is not the first era or culture in which people have expressed hatred for God – this has been going on for a long, long time. (This psalm has been around for several *thousand* years.) But somehow Almighty God, the Creator of the universe, has managed to outlive His critics. They came and went while He just kept on being God. He must not have needed their approval.

In every generation, there will be those who try to stand in opposition to God or attempt to deny His very existence. Of course, those who do so are *invested* heavily in the idea that God doesn't exist because then, if He doesn't, they don't have to be accountable to Him. That mindset is nothing more than a disbelief or a hatred out of convenience, but the day will come when that belief will not be convenient at all.

We have no need to get into an uproar the next time we hear about some militant atheist or anti-Christian group yipping like a horde of angry chihuahuas, trying to advance their agenda. Doesn't the Bible tell us that kind of thing will happen? What did we expect? Too often we respond in anger – not the anger of righteous indignation but an anger ultimately based in fear. This is usually the point at which someone will declare that this whole world is "going to hell in a handbasket!" (whatever that means).

But we don't need to walk in fear. God is not in a panic, wondering how He will deal with our culture. He saw our day coming, and all of the turmoil we see isn't nearly as unique or unprecedented as we might think. God has seen it all already. Remember, there is nothing new under the sun. We serve a great God; and we can be a people of great hope – thrilled to be a small part of what God is doing in our world today. The enemies of God today won't fare any better than His enemies of yesterday who now are gone and forgotten.

HEAD TO HEART

- What do you think is driving the ones who seem to passionately hate God? Why doesn't God simply eliminate them now?

- As lovers of God, how do we respond to haters of God? Or is there a need to respond?

- Does the evil you see in the world today cause you to fear? What is our hope?

DAY 14

WALKING OR STUMBLING?

Whoever is wise, let him understand these things;
whoever is discerning, let him know them;
for the ways of the Lord are right,
and the upright walk in them,
but transgressors stumble in them.

Hosea 14:9

The final verse in the book of Hosea is both powerful and intriguing. Hosea had spent decades prophesying against the spiritual adultery of Israel and the many ways that the people had violated God's commands; but in his final recorded thoughts, Hosea didn't speak about the commandments of God but the *ways* of God instead. Understanding the commandments of God is one thing, but His ways are another matter. Hosea must have forgotten to mention that, although the ways of God are right, they also can be profoundly uncomfortable and far beyond our understanding. Even if he left those specifics out, Hosea was well aware of their reality.

What Hosea endured on a small scale in his personal life was a picture of the spiritual condition of the whole nation of Israel. "When the LORD first spoke through Hosea, the LORD said to Hosea, 'Go, take to yourself a wife of whoredom and have children of whoredom, for the land commits great whoredom by forsaking the LORD'" (Hosea 1:2). The requirement that Hosea marry a prostitute (especially one by the name of *Gomer*) and take her back after she went back into "business" would cause anyone to take a serious look at the ways of God. Yet the conclusion reached by Hosea is that God's ways are right – every one of them. They might be impractical, inconvenient and incomprehensible; but they are right.

Our lives probably don't look anything like Hosea's, but life on this side of heaven inevitably will cause us to deeply ponder God's ways. (If we don't, we'll stay in the realm of pat answers and pop theology, but at least we'll have plenty of company.) What God does or does not do is for God to decide. That includes what He might ask of us and allow to happen in our lives. Not only are His ways higher than our ways, but they simply are *not* our ways. Still, the upright walk in His ways while transgressors stumble in them.

Thankfully, we don't have to understand God's ways to walk in them or even pretend that we're in full agreement; but God invites us into a new level of relationship with Him where His role as God and our role as *not God* are clearly defined. Even if we don't know where we're going or why we're going there, we know who we're following, and walking in His higher ways beats stumbling any day.

HEAD TO HEART

- What is the most challenging thing that God has asked you to do? Did you obey Him in that?

- What are the differences between knowing things about God and knowing His ways?

- What should we do when what God is doing does not make sense to our understanding?

DAY 15

WHAT IF IT DOESN'T MATTER?

*Josiah was eight years old when he began to reign,
and he reigned thirty-one years in Jerusalem. . . .
And he did what was right in the eyes of the LORD
and walked in all the way of David his father, and
he did not turn aside to the right or to the left.*

2 Kings 22:1-2

Once we get past our initial terror at the thought of an eight-year-old being king, we're relieved to see that Josiah grew into the role. Where so many kings of Israel and Judah had served the Lord only halfway and many others not at all, there was no one else like Josiah. Yet as we read the story of Josiah's reign, we might conclude that God chose a strange time for a king like Josiah to rule so righteously and effectively. When Josiah began to rule, Judah was in desperate need of a righteous king; but by the time Josiah could bring a measure of reform, things already had been set irreversibly in motion that could not and would not be turned back. Judgment already was on the way, but let's not get ahead of ourselves.

As a young man, Josiah began to seek the Lord and began the long process of ridding the land of idols and false gods. In the eighteenth year of his reign, the Book of the Law was found, and Josiah realized just how far Judah had departed from what God had commanded. The prophetess Huldah announced that God's judgment on Judah was inevitable but that Josiah would live out his days before His judgment would fall because he had humbled himself before the Lord and acknowledged the wickedness of his nation. (2 Kings 22:14-20)

The amazing thing about Josiah's life is that, knowing all of this, he still proceeded with needed reforms, the removal of idols and the reinstitution of Passover, which had been absent for centuries. He did these things despite knowing that his efforts ultimately would not change the outcome. God's judgment was still coming. No matter what Josiah did, judgment would come once he was out of the picture.

Josiah could have cruised and coasted for the rest of his days and not even attempted to make a difference. He could have done "a King Solomon" and amassed loads of wealth for himself because foregoing his own comfort would not change the outcome in the end. But he didn't. Even though Josiah's life was cut short in battle, he spent his days doing what he could and then he died.

The era of Josiah parallels the current times in some interesting ways. We really do not know exactly what God is going to do or allow to happen; but we can expect that, at some point, God will have had enough. Yes, every other generation lived in wicked times also and expected God's judgment; but our days do have their own distinctions. Although every generation has its "false prophets of doom" who can tell you when, where, why and how God's judgment is going to fall, the truth is that we don't really know. But this doesn't mean we should be naïve enough to expect that things are going to get progressively better. We probably are headed down the road to judgment, and we may very well already be past the point of turning back. It may sound kooky to some, but God's righteousness is not a joke. Just ask Israel and Judah. (2 Kings 17:21-23, 2 Chronicles 36:17-21)

What do we do? The typical response is to groan and gripe. But does that help? All complaining aside, we shouldn't be surprised or act as if we weren't warned about the world being evil. What we can do is to take Josiah's approach. We don't know how long we have or even how effective we can be, but it's better to "make the best use of the time because the days are evil" (Ephesians 5:15) than to sit around cursing the darkness.

God is at work in our day, and He will accomplish His purposes – with or without us. We do well to join with Him because only His purposes will stand. Josiah died and the people of Judah saw God's judgment fall, but undoubtedly Josiah was rewarded for doing what he could do. As it was said of King David, Josiah "served the purpose of God in his own generation" and then he died. Let's do that, too.

HEAD TO HEART

- Do you think the days in which we live are worse than that of previous generations or previous centuries?

- What motivated Josiah to serve the Lord – even though he knew its impact would only be temporary?

- Considering the days in which we live, what does making the best use of the time look like for you?

DAY 16

WAYS AND MEANS

*So Jotham became mighty,
because he ordered his ways before the LORD his God.*

2 Chronicles 27:6

Ecclesiastes tells the sad story of a poor, wise man who, by his wisdom, delivered his city from the oppression of a great king; but no one remembered the poor man. (Ecclesiastes 9:13-16) In the same way, the Bible doesn't tell us a lot about a certain king named Jotham either, but the description we get speaks volumes. Even in the Bible, a lot of notoriety isn't always all it's cracked up to be. But who would not want to have *this* said about us?

If that's a worthy goal, then let's notice a few things about Jotham. First, Jotham presumably had a relationship with Yahweh who was not just the religious figurehead of his community or the God of his ancestors. He was his God, and Jotham must have lived for God's approval. Second, Jotham ordered his ways before the Lord – not just in what he did but in *how* he did it. His motives, his methods, his ambitions and his private thoughts were all in subjection to the Lord; and evidently the Lord was pleased with his ways. The result was that Jotham became mighty.

We can get excited about becoming a person of great strength, but often we're not nearly as excited about what is required to get there. It would be one thing if the process simply involved conformity to certain outward requirements. The problem is religious conformity that is based on outward appearance never has made anyone mighty, but it has made a lot of religious people mean. Often ordering our ways before the Lord is anything but orderly. The process of becoming more like Him is a messy, slow and painful process because our "ways" run a lot deeper than mere behaviors or appearances. Are we willing to take a serious look at our ways and not just our actions? More than that, are we open to the possibility that our ways need to change?

"Search me, O God, and know my heart! Try me and know my thoughts! And see if there be any grievous way in me, and lead me in the way everlasting!" (Psalm 139:23-24)

HEAD TO HEART

- After you are dead and gone, how would you want your life to be summarized?

- How does the Bible's description of strength and might differ from what is valued by the culture?

- In what areas are you tempted to change your outward behavior without looking more deeply in your heart?

DAY 17

JUST KEEP SHOWING UP

"Judgment has come upon the tableland, upon Holon, and Jahzah, and Mephaath, and Dibon, and Nebo, and Beth-diblathaim, and Kiriathaim, and Beth-gamul, and Beth-meon, and Kerioth, and Bozrah, and all the cities of the land of Moab, far and near. The horn of Moab is cut off, and his arm is broken," declares the LORD. "Make him drunk, because he magnified himself against the LORD, so that Moab shall wallow in his vomit, and he too shall be held in derision."

Jeremiah 48:21-26

What we can safely gather from this passage is that Moab is about to really get it. Beyond that, the verses are not overly inspirational. You won't see this one on a calendar or coffee cup. While we safely can conclude that judgment is coming on Moab, everything gets complicated from there. The modern reader and really any reader of the Bible over the centuries probably has no idea where Mephaath is or why Beth-meon is important or if those places even are important beyond a mention in the Bible.

Passages like these demonstrate that God chose to give us a Bible full of references to things that we don't know anything about. He obviously knew we would have no idea where Beth-gamul was or what happened there that caused it to be included in the list of cities that were about to "wallow in" their own "vomit." He gave us a Bible that was not written in our day or our century. God didn't make His Word simplistic or put all of the cookies on the bottom shelf. The Old Testament has entire chapters and sections like this one, which are difficult for us to understand beyond the concept that somebody is about to get whupped.

But it's still worth showing up every day. When we spend time in God's Word, we might not get anything from Beth-meon or Bozrah today; but we still came to the right place for our souls to be nourished, and we never know what we might find tomorrow. *He gave us every part of His Word for a reason; and for that reason, we should read every part of His Word.* This probably wasn't the first passage you haven't fully understood, and it won't be the last; but as we continue to read all of His Word, we will find that – on more days than not – we will come away nourished and refreshed.

HEAD TO HEART

- Are there certain parts of the Bible to which you pay more attention than the others (a canon within the canon)?

- What do you do when you come to portions of Scripture that you don't understand the meaning or even the point?

- Have you ever found new life and truth in the same passage you've read many times before?

DAY 18

ALL OF THE ABOVE

O Lord of hosts, who tests the righteous, who sees the heart and the mind, let me see your vengeance upon them, for to you have I committed my cause. Sing to the Lord; praise the Lord! For he has delivered the life of the needy from the hand of evildoers. Cursed be the day on which I was born! The day when my mother bore me, let it not be blessed! Cursed be the man who brought the news to my father, "A son is born to you," making him very glad.

Jeremiah 20:12-15

Even for an Old Testament prophet, Jeremiah seems to be all over the place with this one. Imagine if this were a multiple-choice question on a test. "Which of the following was said by the prophet Jeremiah?"

(A) Let me see Your vengeance.

(B) Sing praise to the Lord.

(C) Cursed be the day on which I was born or

(D) All of the above.

The answer, of course, is (D) – all of the above. Jeremiah prays for vengeance; he sings praise to the Lord; and then he curses the day on which he was born. Those things don't seem to go together. Since we know Jeremiah's writings likely were compiled later, we don't know for sure when he said each phrase, but the contrast remains and is striking. All of the variety also truly is encouraging.

If we have much experience with being alive in this world, we know that our days often are like that. One moment, we praise the Lord with all of our might; and soon after, we find ourselves angry and depressed. Not only do we pray for justice, but sometimes we also pray for vengeance or wrath. And we know exactly where the wrath of God should be directed.

Before we dismiss Jeremiah as being just immature in his faith, he does have a pretty good track record of faithfulness and obedience. He has an amazing resume of honesty and telling it like it is – even when "like it is" isn't pretty. We never get away from having moments in which we want to "cry for vengeance," nor do we ever escape the frustrations of this life that cause us to question if our lives have any significant meaning. But we can learn to praise the Lord right in the middle of the injustice and darkness because God still is good – even in the moments when life isn't.

HEAD TO HEART

- Are there times when your emotions are all over the place? What are the causes of that?

- Under what circumstances would it be acceptable to pray for God's wrath and vengeance?

- When you pray, does it sound more like a polished, formal prayer or are you "all over the place" like Jeremiah?

DAY 19

HERE TODAY, GONE TOMORROW

Moreover, I saw under the sun that in the place of justice, even there was wickedness, and in the place of righteousness, even there was wickedness. I said in my heart, God will judge the righteous and the wicked, for there is a time for every matter and for every work. I said in my heart with regard to the children of man that God is testing them that they may see that they themselves are but beasts. For what happens to the children of man and what happens to the beasts is the same; as one dies, so dies the other. They all have the same breath, and man has no advantage over the beasts, for all is vanity. All go to one place. All are from the dust, and to dust all return. Who knows whether the spirit of man goes upward and the spirit of the beast goes down into the earth? So I saw that there is nothing better than that a man should rejoice in his work, for that is his lot. Who can bring him to see what will be after him?

Ecclesiastes 3:16-22

Despite amazing medical advances and knowledge unknown to previous generations, the mortality rate still holds steady at 100 percent. No one – good or bad, Christian or atheist, Jew or Gentile, liberal or conservative, carnivore or vegan who was alive 150 years ago – is still alive today. All of them died. From the Old Testament perspective of the Preacher, death is a reminder that "everything is vanity" and death makes man like the beasts who also will all die and return to dust. Not only will we die, but we will live our days with some degree of uncertainty. Things will happen that we don't understand, and things will happen that should not occur.

Although the Preacher was writing under the inspiration of the Holy Spirit, we get to see and know truths on this side of the cross of Jesus that the Preacher did not. If you are the type of person who must have everything figured out, such passages bring humility and perspective. If you are the person who "flies by the seat of your pants" and rarely stops to wonder, this kind of passage causes you to stop and think about the life God has given to you. Today really is quickly fleeting, and eternity is even closer than we know. Are you ready?

Because of Jesus, we might not look forward to *dying*, but we have no reason to fear death. Paul writes, "For if we live, we live to the Lord, and if we die, we die to the Lord. So then, whether we live or whether we die, we are the Lord's" (Romans 14:8). Living or dying, we are His. As Paul also wrote, "For to me to live is Christ, and to die is gain" (Philippians 1:21). Don't get too attached to this world – infinitely better things are on their way.

HEAD TO HEART

- Do you consider it morbid or depressing to contemplate death?

- How often do you think about eternity, and does it affect your daily life?

- What would you do today if you knew it was your last day in this life?

DAY 20

A "BRIEFS" OBJECT LESSON

Thus says the Lord to me, "Go and buy a linen loincloth and put it around your waist, and do not dip it in water." So I bought a loincloth according to the word of the Lord, and put it around my waist. And the word of the Lord came to me a second time, "Take the loincloth that you have bought, which is around your waist, and arise, go to the Euphrates and hide it there in a cleft of the rock... For as the loincloth clings to the waist of a man, so I made the whole house of Israel and the whole house of Judah cling to me," declares the Lord, "that they might be for me a people, a name, a praise, and a glory, but they would not listen."

Jeremiah 13:1-4, 11

While there have been a handful of people who have suggested that object lessons are out of place in a sermon or Bible teaching, God used an object lesson with Jeremiah, so those people are apparently wrong. At the same time, if people remember the object lesson but don't remember its point, then it's nothing more than a distraction. But God used Jeremiah's loincloth, of all things, to convey His message to Jeremiah and then to His people. What then can be learned from Jeremiah's underwear, and was he able to keep it *brief*? (Groan.)

If nothing else, knowing that underwear really hasn't changed much since the days of Jeremiah is amusing. They probably would have been amazed with the elastic waistbands we take for granted, but still the loincloth was to serve the same purpose – to cling around a person's waist. But still, God gave Jeremiah a strange object lesson. Even for an Old Testament prophet, being told to go and hide your underwear in a cleft of the rock was unusual. Naturally, the loincloth deteriorated there and became worthless. It was supposed to cling; but it wasn't clingy any longer and, therefore, was useless.

What was the lesson of the underwear that wouldn't cling? The loincloth was a representation of God's people. Once the loincloth was hidden away, it was ruined. It would not cling – just as the people would not cling to the Lord. In the same way, we were created to be a people for His praise and His glory. That is possible only when we cling tightly to Him, knowing that God is really the One who is holding on to us. Even our underwear can serve to remind us of that. If they don't, it's probably time to go shopping.

(Quick side note: This passage gives new meaning to Isaiah 30:4: "Though they have officials in Zoan and their envoys have arrived in *Hanes*.")

HEAD TO HEART

- Have you ever sensed the Holy Spirit leading you to do something that seemed strange to you?

- Why do you think God used such a lesson to convey His point rather than simply saying that His people were not listening?

- In what specific ways are we to cling to the Lord? What happens as we do?

DAY 21

THE PURSUIT OF NOTHING

*The words of the Preacher,
the son of David, king in Jerusalem.*

*Vanity of vanities, says the Preacher,
vanity of vanities! All is vanity.
What does man gain by all the toil
at which he toils under the sun?
A generation goes, and a generation comes,
but the earth remains forever.
The sun rises, and the sun goes down,
and hastens to the place where it rises. . . .*

*I the Preacher have been king over Israel in Jerusalem.
And I applied my heart to seek and to search out by wisdom
all that is done under heaven.
It is an unhappy business that God has given
to the children of man to be busy with. I have seen
everything that is done under the sun, and behold,
all is vanity and a striving after wind.*

*What is crooked cannot be made straight,
and what is lacking cannot be counted. I said in my heart,
"I have acquired great wisdom,
surpassing all who were over Jerusalem before me,
and my heart has had great
experience of wisdom and knowledge."
And I applied my heart to know wisdom
and to know madness and folly.
I perceived that this also is but a striving after wind.
For in much wisdom is much vexation,
and he who increases knowledge increases sorrow.*

Ecclesiastes 1:1-5, 12-18

As we first read the thoughts of the Preacher (believed to be Solomon), we might wonder why he was having such a bad day or if he had not had his coffee yet. Such thoughts never would land the Preacher a slot in the self-help section at the local bookstore. But we automatically know he isn't wrong because Ecclesiastes is Scripture. If we've spent some years on the planet, these truths resonate with our experience as well.

Many of us know the futility of passionately chasing after worthless things in this world and have experienced the sinking feeling of reaching a goal or achieving our ambition – only to find ourselves still unfulfilled. We strive and labor to reach the top or at least what we believe that to be. Whether it's a title to hold, an accomplishment or some special knowledge, we can be deceived into believing if we just had "that," then we finally could be happy.

But the Preacher, who held a position of power and possessed incredible wisdom and vast wealth, described it all as vanity and a striving after the wind. Devoting time and energy with the motive of making a name for ourselves is a wasted pursuit just as it was for the builders of the Tower of Babel. (See Genesis 11.)

Try as we might to make a name for ourselves, we will be forgotten soon after we're gone. Why is that not depressing? Because remembering our frailty gives us perspective on what matters and what doesn't. We never will find fulfillment and satisfaction in so many of our pursuits because God did not create us to be satisfied by those things. He has created us in a way that we are unfulfilled by the things of the world so that we will find our joy in Him. Experiencing the meaninglessness and futility in this life reminds us we have a much better life awaiting us.

This doesn't mean all those things must be avoided if we recognize that none of them will make a very good god. When God is the ultimate in our lives, then we can enjoy His blessings for His glory. When we try to enjoy the blessings for their own sake apart from Him, we make them false wells that quickly or eventually run dry. As the great missionary William Carey once said, "I'm not afraid of failure. I'm afraid of succeeding at things that don't matter." Few, if any of us, will ever get to see life from the Preacher's point of view; but we can take his word for it. Are we living as servants of Christ or chasing vanity and striving after the wind?

HEAD TO HEART

- In what ways have you experienced the vanity of life described by the Preacher?

- Have you ever accomplished a goal or reached a great milestone and found it still doesn't satisfy your heart?

- How do we know what pleasures we can enjoy and what needs we should set aside?

DAY 22

TODAY IS THE DAY

This is the day that the LORD has made;
let us rejoice and be glad in it.

Psalm 118:24

Have you ever noticed when you're having a rotten day that often someone comes along and makes it worse? Noticing that you're down, they somehow feel obligated to attempt encouragement. Just as we are feeling content in our misery and justified in our grumbling, someone spouts, *"This is the day that the LORD has made; let us rejoice and be glad in it."* The people who do that never realize how close they came to death in those moments. A word fitly spoken is better than saying the right thing at the wrong time.

But are they wrong to quote Scripture? Of course not. Shouldn't we rejoice and be thankful every day? Definitely. But we don't always want to because complaining and seeing ourselves as victims is easier. While such well-meaning people can soar to new heights on the "annoying scale" when they rush to point out what we don't want to hear in the moment, the truth of the Scripture is not at all diminished: *"This is the day that the LORD has made; let us rejoice and be glad in it."*

It's possible for a verse of Scripture to become so familiar to us or quoted so frequently *at* us that we fail to see its significance; but the days in which we live require us to either remember that God is in control, or we will give in to grumbling and despair. Have you noticed that plenty of people seem to be really angry these days? What's the source of all that anger? Many times the driving force behind the anger is actually fear. Whenever we face circumstances that are beyond our control, we become fearful, and the fear can escalate quickly to the state of fighting mad – even if we don't fully know why. The circumstances are, in fact, beyond our control; so what do we do?

This verse in Psalms is not a band-aid to apply to life's hurts. Scripture addresses the anger and the fear; and carefully considered, we see the sovereignty and wonder of God when we choose to see today as the day that God made and we begin to realize all that this entails. *This is the day that the LORD has made* means that *God* made the day. While seemingly obvious, the significance of that truth is tremendous: God made the day, so He also rules the day. He is totally in control of what happens.

Because God made the day and rules the day, we are never hapless victims. Our days do not consist of random, chaotic events that just sort of happen. We are not defined by what happens to us but by the One to whom we belong. He is actively ruling and reigning over all of His creation, and each day has purpose and significance for His glory and for our good.

This is the day that the LORD has made also points to the importance of today because it's the only day we have. Yesterday is over, and tomorrow is not guaranteed. God made today, so today matters. The events of today may seem totally unimportant, yet today matters because it is the only day that God has given to us. We can't change what happened yesterday, and we can't do anything about tomorrow. We only have the day called today.

Today is the only day we have in which to rejoice and be glad. If we are not thankful today, then we really won't be tomorrow either. If we will not rejoice and be glad today, we'll simply continue to complain tomorrow the way we did today. Let's remind ourselves (so that annoying person won't even have the opportunity) that every day is His day, so we can choose to rejoice and be glad.

HEAD TO HEART

- Have you ever received "encouragement" that wasn't encouraging at all?

- How do you know when it's the right time to encourage someone and when it is not?

- What difference does it make in your outlook and perspective that God made the day we are living?

DAY 23

BARREN, BROKEN AND BLESSED

There was a certain man of Ramathaim-zophim of the hill country of Ephraim whose name was Elkanah... He had two wives. The name of the one was Hannah, and the name of the other, Peninnah. And Peninnah had children, but Hannah had no children.

1 Samuel 1:1-2

Have you ever noticed that God is not all that concerned about doing things your way? The Lord is intent on advancing His agenda even if those plans do not meet with our approval. God is evidently more interested in His glory than ours. This is never more clearly indicated than in the life of Hannah.

Hannah was barren, which was neither her fault nor her choosing. To make a bad situation worse, her husband's *other* wife was bearing children for him. It also didn't help that "wife number two" would taunt Hannah since the infertility obviously could not be blamed on the man. More than that, infertility was not seen as a medical issue at that time but as an indication of God's disfavor. All the way around, it was an ordeal as Hannah bore the stigma of rejection and family dysfunction. God *could* have opened Hannah's womb before it ever reached this point, and Hannah *could* have enjoyed a normal marriage that produced normal offspring; but God often works in ways that aren't normal.

One husband, two wives and an intense rivalry undoubtedly would have created a measure of tension in their marriage. "And Elkanah, her husband, said to her, 'Hannah, why do you weep? And why do you not eat? And why is your heart sad? Am I not more to you than ten sons?'" (1 Samuel 1:8) (What do you bet that really wasn't the right thing to say?) It quickly became a situation that only God could fix; and if God didn't do something, Hannah faced a life full of misery. So Hannah kept praying and praying. It became obvious that only God could fix this situation, but that's just the kind of situation that God evidently loves to fix.

No, a long and tearful season of waiting wasn't what Hannah (or her husband Elkanah) would have chosen; but God was at work doing His own thing in His own way. And what He was doing was more than they could have asked or imagined. The circumstances were especially difficult because God was doing a special work. In His timing and in His way, God chose these circumstances to bring about the birth of the prophet Samuel; and as Samuel's life and ministry would demonstrate, this was a special child. Since God could have granted them a son long before, no one would ever be able to convince them that Samuel's birth was anything less than miraculous.

Yours may or may not be the desire for a child; but as you consider the desires of your own heart, be encouraged. Maybe God has not yet answered your cries because He is going to do a Samuel-like work in your life; and when the answer comes, it will be obvious that God did what only God can do. God answered Hannah's prayer for a child, but this work was much bigger than a couple having a child. The Lord was raising up Samuel the prophet, one of the most significant figures in the entire Old Testament.

You may be weary of waiting; you may be discouraged; and you may even be angry; but maybe God is doing something that only He can do that is much bigger than you would ever have expected. God still gives "Samuels," and He still grants them in His time and in His way.

HEAD TO HEART

- What is the "Samuel" for which you are praying to God?
- Knowing that God could answer your prayer immediately, how do you deal with the discouragement that can accompany having to wait?
- Do you think that Hannah would have continued to serve the Lord had the answer been a no? Would you?

DAY 24

THE CURSE OF AN EASY ROAD

Now King Solomon loved many foreign women... Solomon clung to these in love. He had 700 wives, princesses, and 300 concubines. And his wives turned away his heart. For when Solomon was old his wives turned away his heart after other gods, and his heart was not wholly true to the Lord his God, as was the heart of David his father... So Solomon did what was evil in the sight of the Lord and did not wholly follow the Lord, as David his father had done.

1 Kings 11:1-6

Having 700 wives and 300 concubines is simply a bad idea, and there at least that many reasons why; but it probably is wise not to mention all of them here. One of the great ironies of this passage is that Solomon was gifted with great *wisdom*, but he acted the fool on a huge scale in this area of his life. The worst part of Solomon's escapades is that his wives ended up turning his heart away from the Lord. The saga of Solomon wasn't just a man misbehaving or acting out a mid-life crisis – his heart was led away.

It's interesting that the Bible says Solomon's heart was not true to the Lord as his father David's had been, especially since David had his own issues with adultery. After all, Solomon's mother was Bathsheba, the very woman with whom David had sinned. While David had an episode of dramatic failure in his life, what separates David from Solomon is that apparently David's heart was never led away – even when his actions were deplorable. Long after David was dead and gone, the Bible still spoke of him as being a man after God's own heart. (Acts 13:22) When David was confronted and finally came clean concerning what he had done, we see a broken, humble and penitent man. (Psalm 51) Solomon simply continued the same downward spiral. What can we learn from their lives and their failures?

If we consider the lives of David and Solomon, we notice huge differences between the father and the son. Perhaps what stands out the most is that David's life was never easy, especially when he was younger, while everything seemed to fall into place for Solomon. We might envy Solomon for that, but none of us would want our lives to turn out like his. So what happened to Solomon?

First, Solomon had no battles to fight – he simply inherited the kingship. Unlike David, he never had a spear thrown at him and never had to flee for his life because of a jealous king. Solomon probably never tended sheep or fought off a bear and a lion. Solomon likely never perceived the need to learn to trust in the Lord because his path was an easy one, but David had learned to trust the Lord because his circumstances required a strong faith again and again.

Secondly, Solomon had the whole world to tell him how wise and wonderful he was. People came from all over just to listen to his wisdom. That does wonders for an ego but not necessarily good wonders. Soon the praises of people go to a person's head. In contrast, David had experienced the sting of rejection – even from his own family. When the prophet came to anoint the next king from among the sons of Jesse, David was completely disregarded and left to tend the sheep. Solomon never knew such rejection – he was destined to be king from the start.

Possibly the most catastrophic difference between David and Solomon was the role of accountability. The first two kings of Israel had a prophet of the Lord to confront them when they did wrong. King Saul had Samuel, King David had Nathan; but there doesn't seem to be anyone there for King Solomon when he started down a destructive path. He did what he wanted when he wanted, and no one was there to tell him otherwise. Sadly, he lacked the wisdom to surround himself with people who could tell him no. That is precisely how a wise man ends up with 700 wives and 300 concubines.

Failure is a wonderful teacher. Many times, we can even learn from someone else's mistakes instead of suffering the consequences ourselves. What can we learn from Solomon's failures? First, we can rejoice that God uses the trials, battles and struggles to build the character and integrity we need to finish well. We might wish for an easier road than the one God has assigned, but the easy path won't get us where we want to go.

We also do well to see that our jealousies are often misplaced. The things we might consider to be advantages and blessings in the lives of others aren't always that. Gifts and abilities are useless if they end up contributing to our failure. Finally, we need to let a handful of people get close enough to us that they can speak into our lives when a rebuke is needed. None of us are exempt from making a mess of our lives to the very same degree of both David and Solomon. In the end, however, may we be known as men and women after God's own heart.

HEAD TO HEART

- Have you been secretly (or not so secretly) jealous of someone because it seems as though their path is so much easier than yours?

- From what struggles and adversities in your life have you grown the most? Would you change them now if you could?

- Who do you have in your life that can tell you that you're wrong? Whose counsel will you truly heed?

DAY 25

WORK, WORK, WORK

I hated all my toil in which I toil under the sun, seeing that I must leave it to the man who will come after me, and who knows whether he will be wise or a fool? Yet he will be master of all for which I toiled and used my wisdom under the sun. This also is vanity. So I turned about and gave my heart up to despair over all the toil of my labors under the sun, because sometimes a person who has toiled with wisdom and knowledge and skill must leave everything to be enjoyed by someone who did not toil for it. This also is vanity and a great evil. What has a man from all the toil and striving of heart with which he toils beneath the sun? For all his days are full of sorrow, and his work is a vexation. Even in the night his heart does not rest. This also is vanity. There is nothing better for a person than that he should eat and drink and find enjoyment in his toil. This also, I saw, is from the hand of God, for apart from him who can eat or who can have enjoyment? For to the one who pleases him God has given wisdom and knowledge and joy, but to the sinner he has given the business of gathering and collecting, only to give to one who pleases God. This also is vanity and a striving after wind.

Ecclesiastes 2:18-26

What would you do if it became no longer necessary to work at your current job? If retirement were an option for you financially, would you retire today? Many view retirement as the ultimate goal – only to discover they are bored and run out of things to do when the time finally comes for retirement. We can be tempted to believe that, if only we did not have to work, we could find fulfillment and enjoyment in life. But we were created to work and to be productive. That doesn't mean we always love our jobs or won't experience futility as we do our jobs, but our existence is intended to be more than taking up space.

Maybe you've heard the legend of Sisyphus, and perhaps you can relate. Sisyphus received a terrible punishment. Every day he had to roll a huge rock up a steep hill with the goal of finally bringing the rock to rest at the top. But every day, just as he reached the top, the rock would slip and roll all the way down the hill again. Someone modernized this legend and compared it to a data entry job. Every morning the person begins entering data into a computer and does so all day long. They anxiously await the five o'clock hour when their work is saved and archived; but every day, at 4:55, someone trips over the power cord and the entire day's work is lost – again. This is part of what "subjected to futility" means. (Romans 8:20)

Work itself was not a part of the curse of sin, but *toil* certainly was. Punishing and arduous labor, with little or no result, is part of the futility to which creation is subjected – for now. If you enjoy what you do for a living, be grateful for the opportunity and how God uses your job to provide. If you are miserable in your employment, seek the Lord, His wisdom and certainly His timing. It may be time for a change, or this may very well be one of the ways God will refine you and train you. Finally, in all we do, the most important thing is to remember whom we ultimately are serving. God knows. God sees. "And whatever you do, in word or deed, do everything in the name of the Lord Jesus, giving thanks to God the Father through him" (Colossians 3:17).

HEAD TO HEART

- Do you feel called to do your current job, or does it simply pay the bills?

- What job or role would others consider to be "work" that would be a joy for you to do?

- How can you glorify God through your vocation?

DAY 26

FOLLOW THE PILLAR

When Pharaoh let the people go, God did not lead them by way of the land of the Philistines, although that was near. For God said, "Lest the people change their minds when they see war and return to Egypt." But God led the people around by the way of the wilderness toward the Red Sea. And the people of Israel went up out of the land of Egypt equipped for battle.... And the LORD went before them by day in a pillar of cloud to lead them along the way, and by night in a pillar of fire to give them light, that they might travel by day and by night. The pillar of cloud by day and the pillar of fire by night did not depart from before the people.

Exodus 13:17-18, 21-22

If we are seeking to follow and serve the Lord, we are making the effort to ensure that we are where God wants us to be. Sometimes we wonder if we should stay or if the time has come to move on to a new job, new friends, a new church and on it goes. Being where God wants us to be is essential, but sometimes knowing where we aren't supposed to be is much clearer than where we are. For the people of Israel journeying in the wilderness, the Lord made it easy to know where and when He was leading them. His guidance wasn't complicated – just follow the pillar, and you'll be right where God wants you to be. Chasing a pillar around sounds like a great arrangement – at least if all we really want from God are directions to His blessings. Following the pillar, you would know which way to go every time. You could follow the pillar with everyone else or not follow the pillar and go it alone. The options would be limited, but at least you would know. You wouldn't need much of a relationship with God for that.

But truly living by the power and direction of the Holy Spirit rarely resembles following a pillar. Often we don't have as much clarity and direction as we would like, but that's usually because we want to know *right now* instead of waiting on God and walking with God. The Lord will make His will and His way known in His timing; but in the waiting and seasons of our indecision, we get to know Him and experience His presence. The people of Israel had the pillar to guide them; but as they would demonstrate regularly, they didn't really know God. Certainly, we want to know His leading and His direction – but not without knowing Him in the process. A pillar, even one we can see, just isn't the same.

HEAD TO HEART

- Do you sometimes feel as though God could be much clearer in revealing His will to you?

- If God is not going to provide a pillar for you, how can you posture yourself to hear from the Lord when He is making known His will?

- Does your prayer life reveal more desire for answers or for a relationship with God?

DAY 27

WHEN THE KING IS DEAD

In the year that King Uzziah died I saw the Lord sitting upon a throne, high and lifted up; and the train of his robe filled the temple. Above him stood the seraphim. Each had six wings: with two he covered his face, and with two he covered his feet, and with two he flew. And one called to another and said: "Holy, holy, holy is the LORD of hosts; the whole earth is full of his glory!"

Isaiah 6:1-3

Think back to the final moments of the previous year or the first day of the new year. The end of one year and the beginning of another are always interesting times. For many, the anticipation of a new year is accompanied with the determination that *this* year will be different; but usually, the new year – with all of its resolutions and commitments – turns out to be no different than the previous year and all the ones before. No, the changing of the calendar doesn't automatically result in a change in the circumstances or the person. In considering the days and years of our lives, what is our hope? Do we trust in our determination or willpower or level of commitment? Will things inevitably get better simply because we hope they will?

When Isaiah saw the Lord, it was no coincidence it happened in the year that Uzziah died. God was giving Isaiah this vision to remind him of a colossal truth considering all that Isaiah would face as the prophet of the Lord. King Uzziah was dead. After a prosperous reign of 52 years and relative stability in Judah, the good, old days were all over.

To make matters worse, Uzziah's reign and his life didn't end well. His success apparently went to his head and caused him to become prideful. Uzziah had taken it upon himself to burn incense in the temple of the

Lord even though only the priests were assigned and consecrated to this role. Uzziah raged against the priests who confronted him; and even as he ranted and raved, leprosy broke out on his forehead. He had leprosy to the day he died. He lived separately from his household, and his son effectively stepped in for him – even though he was still living. Things didn't end well. So now the good, old days under Uzziah were over; and the last years of his life cast a shadow over the good years. (2 Chronicles 26:16-23)

The good days under King Uzziah were gone. Comfort and prosperity were replaced with uncertainty and insecurity for Isaiah and the people of Judah. Yet, in the year that King Uzziah died, Isaiah saw the Lord. Even though the king was dead, *the King* was still reigning on His throne. What Isaiah needed to see the most in this moment was that God still was firmly seated on His throne – exalted over everything. In times of turmoil, instability and insecurity, let's rest and rejoice in the same assurance. Thousands of years and many other kings later, God still is reigning on His throne.

Our hope, in a new year and on every new day, is rooted in understanding that the King is alive and is still in complete control. We will fail, but He won't. For good or bad, our circumstances will change, but He won't. May we face each day and every year we are granted with hearts full of hope, not in ourselves or in our circumstances, but in our King.

HEAD TO HEART

- As we saw Isaiah's world being shaken, how has your world been shaken recently?

- Are you sometimes overwhelmed with current events and the instability of your circumstances? How do you handle this?

- What can we learn from what happened to Uzziah? How do we handle success in a way that honors God?

DAY 28

THE BORING HERO

And the people of Israel did what was evil in the sight of the LORD. They forgot the LORD their God and served the Baals and the Asheroth. Therefore the anger of the LORD was kindled against Israel, and he sold them into the hand of Cushan-rishathaim king of Mesopotamia. And the people of Israel served Cushan-rishathaim eight years. But when the people of Israel cried out to the LORD, the LORD raised up a deliverer for the people of Israel, who saved them, Othniel the son of Kenaz, Caleb's younger brother. The Spirit of the LORD was upon him, and he judged Israel. He went out to war, and the LORD gave Cushan-rishathaim king of Mesopotamia into his hand. And his hand prevailed over Cushan-rishathaim. So the land had rest forty years. Then Othniel the son of Kenaz died.

Judges 3:7–11

Maybe you've never heard of a Bible hero named Othniel. Although he was the first judge mentioned in the book of Judges, he is definitely not the best known. The judges in the Old Testament were not judicial officials with a robe and gavel in the way that we think of a judge today. They were men and women who God raised up to rescue His people from their oppressors. In a book full of characters and exciting stories, Othniel often is overlooked because he is not particularly exciting – just highly effective. As far as we know, he had no glaring weakness or incredible strength. He was not left-handed like Ehud or a woman like Deborah. Othniel was simply faithful and obedient.

If Othniel had a claim to fame, he was the nephew of the legendary Caleb. Not too exciting, and yet Othniel was used by God to bring about deliverance for Israel. The oppression they had endured for eight years now was replaced by peace for the next 40. The Spirit of the Lord was upon him and gave him great success. And then he died. That's all we are told, but the story of Othniel still instructs us.

There probably will never be a movie made based on the life of Othniel, but God used him to do great things. Too often we are looking for something exciting or at least fulfilling in service to the Lord, but that should not be the criteria. What does matter is that we are serving the Lord. It's not always glamorous or exciting, and we don't always get recognized or appreciated for what we do. That didn't stop Othniel; and even though his story may not be the most exciting, everything that is said about him is favorable. That certainly can't be said about many other more famous Bible characters. May we be faithful to God's calling for us even if we are "a little boring" like Othniel because there will be nothing boring about a rich reward in heaven.

HEAD TO HEART

- Why do you think the Bible gives many details about some characters and few about others?

- Do you know anyone who, like Othniel, quietly and faithfully serves the Lord and His people?

- Having read the brief legacy of Othniel, what will be the legacy of your life?

DAY 29

USING WHAT IS LEFT

Then the people of Israel cried out to the LORD, and the LORD raised up for them a deliverer, Ehud, the son of Gera, the Benjaminite, a left-handed man. The people of Israel sent tribute by him to Eglon the king of Moab. And Ehud made for himself a sword with two edges, a cubit in length, and he bound it on his right thigh under his clothes. And he presented the tribute to Eglon king of Moab. Now Eglon was a very fat man. . . . And Ehud reached with his left hand, took the sword from his right thigh, and thrust it into his belly. And the hilt also went in after the blade, and the fat closed over the blade, for he did not pull the sword out of his belly; and the dung came out. . . .So Moab was subdued that day under the hand of Israel. And the land had rest for eighty years.

Judges 3:15-30

One of the ways that we know the Bible is true is that you just can't make up things like this. God raised up the left-handed Ehud to deliver His people. That may not seem strange to us; but in those days, the right hand represented strength. A person who was left handed generally was considered defective. It may be that Ehud was a lefty only because he had a deformity or at least did not have the full use of his right hand. But whether Ehud was just naturally left handed or if there was an issue with his right hand, limitations and perceived handicaps have never been a problem for the Lord.

In fact, Ehud used what others considered a weakness to his own advantage. King Eglon would not have suspected a threat coming from Ehud's left hand, and this is likely part of the reason the Moabite king would let an Israelite get so close to him – close enough to harpoon him with a dagger. The dagger in the left hand evidently was thrust into just the right spot. And just like that, Ehud killed King Eglon, the oppressor of Israel, and set in motion the deliverance of Israel from the Moabites. Peace was hard to come by in the days of the judges, but this peace lasted for 80 years.

Many people would be surprised to find a funny story with such gory details in the Bible, but we see such graphic details here and in other passages as well. The story of Ehud serves as a reminder that God can use anyone He wants, however He wants. We also see that the Creator of humor has a great sense of humor. The things we perceive to be our greatest weaknesses put no limitations on what God can do. Are we wholly available to Him – strengths, weaknesses and all?

HEAD TO HEART

- What do you consider to be your limitations or weaknesses?

- Why does the Lord often use a seemingly weak person or the weakness in a person – rather than strength – to accomplish His purposes?

- Are you available for God to use you in whatever way He would choose?

DAY 30

WHEN THE GLORY ISN'T YOURS

Now Deborah, a prophetess, the wife of Lappidoth, was judging Israel at that time. She used to sit under the palm of Deborah between Ramah and Bethel in the hill country of Ephraim, and the people of Israel came up to her for judgment. She sent and summoned Barak the son of Abinoam from Kedesh-naphtali and said to him, "Has not the LORD, the God of Israel, commanded you, "Go, gather your men at Mount Tabor, taking 10,000 from the people of Naphtali and the people of Zebulun. And I will draw out Sisera, the general of Jabin's army, to meet you by the river Kishon with his chariots and his troops, and I will give him into your hand?" Barak said to her, "If you will go with me, I will go, but if you will not go with me, I will not go." And she said, "I will surely go with you. Nevertheless, the road on which you are going will not lead to your glory, for the LORD will sell Sisera into the hand of a woman." Then Deborah arose and went with Barak to Kedesh.

Judges 4:4-9

If you aren't familiar with the book of Judges, Judges 4 probably would present you with surprises, especially by how the enemy of Israel is eliminated. Let's just say he was no longer a "headache" for the people of Israel. (Judges 4:17-23) Deborah is the only female judge in the book of Judges; and although we are not given a great deal of information about her, we learn that her wisdom and counsel were sought after among the people of Israel.

Barak evidently recognized Deborah's value when he refused to go into war without her. This conversation between Deborah and Barak is an interesting one, and we can understand their dialogue in more than one way. When Barak said he would not enter the battle if she would not go with him, that could be taken as weakness on his part, but maybe it isn't. Deborah responded that she would go but wanted Barak to understand that "the road on which you are going will not lead to your glory." At first, this sounds like a rebuke and that Barak is on the wrong road.

But Deborah's warning could be taken another way. Barak was doing what God had said to do and did go into battle as instructed. Deborah simply wanted him to understand that the glory of victory would not be his, but Barak still engaged in battle. Deborah said the glory would go to a woman, but she wasn't referring to herself. We see later that the woman was named Jael, and she wasn't even in the battle. Barak and his army won a great victory, leaving only the enemy commander to escape – until Jael drove a tent peg through his head! Barak did win the battle, but someone else got the glory.

What if we never get any glory for what we do? Would we still make the same effort? This is a great test of our true motivation. Barak still was obedient – even when he knew the glory would not be his. May we have the same attitude as we serve the Lord and serve one another.

HEAD TO HEART

- What are the things that truly motivate people to take on a significant challenge?

- What would you do differently if you knew there would be no recognition or appreciation for doing it?

- Who is the "Deborah" in your life, the one without whom you would not want to go into battle?

DAY 31

NOT HOW BUT WHO

When Sisera was told that Barak the son of Abinoam had gone up to Mount Tabor, Sisera called out all his chariots, 900 chariots of iron, and all the men who were with him, from Harosheth-hagoyim to the river Kishon. And Deborah said to Barak, "Up! For this is the day in which the LORD has given Sisera into your hand. Does not the LORD go out before you?" So Barak went down from Mount Tabor with 10,000 men following him. And the LORD routed Sisera and all his chariots and all his army before Barak by the edge of the sword. And Sisera got down from his chariot and fled away on foot. And Barak pursued the chariots and the army to Harosheth-hagoyim, and all the army of Sisera fell by the edge of the sword; not a man was left.

Judges 4:12-16

Before this section of Judges 4, we learn that Israel was being oppressed by Sisera's army and their 900 chariots. The army of Israel, led by Barak, was no match for the Canaanite army and had no chariots to match the Canaanites. But the battle wasn't a fair fight because God was fighting for the Israelites. Barak and his army went and routed the Canaanite army. How could Israel win such an apparently easy battle against an opponent with 900 chariots?

The Bible doesn't really tell us how they won the battle – just that they did. The story goes from a formidable foe to a routed enemy almost instantly. Obviously, the Lord was fighting for Israel to allow them to defeat the army with all of their chariots but not until later do we find out how this happened. Judges 5 records the victorious song of Deborah and Barak, but the celebration song also reveals how God gave victory to the army of Israel. Judges 5:4 says, "LORD, when you went out from Seir, when you marched from the region of Edom, the earth trembled and the heavens dropped, yes, the clouds dropped water." Did you catch what happened? God sent rain, and 900 chariots don't work well in the mud. In fact, they only get stuck and become vulnerable to attack.

This is another example that nothing is too hard for the Lord. The very things that seem to be insurmountable obstacles are easily overcome when the battle belongs to the Lord. We may not see how, and we may not even see a way forward; but He goes before us and fights for us. He is working in ways that we don't see until later.

HEAD TO HEART

- What are the obstacles that seem insurmountable in your life right now?

- Why might God have sent rain to help the army of Israel rather than simply making the army of Israel more powerful and effective?

- For what battle or obstacle is God calling you to trust Him today?

DAY 32

BUT WE DIDN'T ASK FOR THAT

The people of Israel did what was evil in the sight of the LORD, and the LORD gave them into the hand of Midian seven years. ... And Israel was brought very low because of Midian. And the people of Israel cried out for help to the LORD. When the people of Israel cried out to the LORD on account of the Midianites, the LORD sent a prophet to the people of Israel. And he said to them, "Thus says the LORD, the God of Israel: I led you up from Egypt and brought you out of the house of slavery. And I delivered you from the hand of the Egyptians and from the hand of all who oppressed you, and drove them out before you and gave you their land. And I said to you, 'I am the LORD your God; you shall not fear the gods of the Amorites in whose land you dwell.' But you have not obeyed my voice."

Judges 6:1-10

Up until this point in Judges, when the people of Israel were oppressed, they cried out to the Lord, and he would raise up a deliverer. But not this time. When the people cried out in their oppression, God did not raise up a deliverer – He sent a prophet. The problem was that no one had asked for a prophet. They just wanted God to come through and rescue them again – just as He had done in previous times. In their minds, that was God's job.

The inconvenient truth we see in this is that God often will give us what we *need* instead of (or at least before) He gives us what we ask. The people of Israel needed to be confronted with the truth of *why* they were in such a bad situation before there was any hope of being rescued from their oppression. They had brought this condition on themselves – again. God would later raise up Gideon to bring deliverance, but this would be the last warning and the deliverance only would be temporary.

God sent a prophet to speak the truth of their disobedience in a time where everyone truly was doing what was right in his own eyes. (Judges 21:25) To the people of Israel at that time and to so many today, everyone doing what is right in their own eyes sounds liberating, but "right in their own eyes" does the opposite. Disobedience and doing only what we want leads to oppression and slavery in one form or another, which the people of Israel never seemed to learn. None of us possess the wisdom to be able to do whatever we want all of the time. In His mercy, God confronts us with the truth – often at the times when we least want to listen. Often the times we want God to act are the times when He is ready to speak. Are we even listening?

HEAD TO HEART

- When was the last time you were confronted with the truth and didn't like it at all?

- Why would God continue to rescue the people of Israel when they kept getting back into the same situation repeatedly?

- Why is everyone doing what is right in their own eyes such a bad idea?

DAY 33

THE HIDING WARRIOR

Now the angel of the LORD came and sat under the terebinth at Ophrah, which belonged to Joash the Abiezrite, while his son Gideon was beating out wheat in the winepress to hide it from the Midianites. And the angel of the LORD appeared to him and said to him, "The LORD is with you, O mighty man of valor." And Gideon said to him, "Please, my lord, if the LORD is with us, why then has all this happened to us? And where are all his wonderful deeds that our fathers recounted to us, saying, 'Did not the LORD bring us up from Egypt?' But now the LORD has forsaken us and given us into the hand of Midian." And the LORD turned to him and said, "Go in this might of yours and save Israel from the hand of Midian; do not I send you?" And he said to him, "Please, Lord, how can I save Israel? Behold, my clan is the weakest in Manasseh, and I am the least in my father's house." And the LORD said to him, "But I will be with you, and you shall strike the Midianites as one man."

Judges 6:11-16

One of the perks of being omniscient is that God can see what someone will be even when they are clearly not living up to it in the present. When the angel of the Lord called Gideon a "mighty man of valor," Gideon was anything but that in his own eyes and likely in the eyes of others. Mighty men of valor don't typically hide when they are working, but Gideon did. They also don't make excuses when they are given the opportunity to do something great; but Gideon did that, too.

But this was not about God knowing exceptional talent when He saw it. In many ways, Gideon was right about himself. He didn't meet the expected criteria for a deliverer. He also didn't display much faith in the Lord. He even blamed God for the natural consequences of Israel's idolatry. In a worldly sense, there were probably lots of people more qualified than Gideon. Like Moses had done many years before, Gideon offered multiple excuses and suggested that God must be mistaken in selecting him.

So why did God see Gideon in the manner He did? God could see that Gideon would be a mighty man of valor because, at the same time, He was promising to Gideon, "I will be with you." As the story of Gideon would play out, only Yahweh's presence and power could bring about the kind of victory that Gideon would lead. Our gifts and abilities are blessings and often helpful, but the source of our strength is the living and abiding presence of God in our lives. What we attempt to do for the Lord in our strength or wisdom will accomplish nothing, but there are no limits to what God can do through us as we rely and depend upon Him.

HEAD TO HEART

- Are you relying on the Lord or your abilities?

- Why does God sometimes use the most unlikely people – even when they are resistant to His will?

- How does what God says about you differ from what you would say about yourself?

DAY 34

FIRST THINGS FIRST

Then Gideon built an altar there to the LORD and called it, The LORD Is Peace. To this day it still stands at Ophrah, which belongs to the Abiezrites. That night the LORD said to him, "Take your father's bull, and the second bull seven years old, and pull down the altar of Baal that your father has, and cut down the Asherah that is beside it and build an altar to the LORD your God on the top of the stronghold here, with stones laid in due order. Then take the second bull and offer it as a burnt offering with the wood of the Asherah that you shall cut down." So Gideon took ten men of his servants and did as the LORD had told him. But because he was too afraid of his family and the men of the town to do it by day, he did it by night.

Judges 6:24-27

Gideon wasn't easily convinced that God was indeed calling him to be the human instrument of deliverance for the Israelites from the oppression of Midian. But if Gideon was ready to charge into battle, the time to fight had not yet arrived. Before he was ready to deal with the Midianites, Gideon had to first deal with his household. God had not chosen Gideon because his family was free of idols, but God was commanding him to first deal with the idolatry in his home. Even though he was afraid and acted under the cover of darkness, Gideon was obedient to God and willing to face the consequences among his people. When Gideon destroyed their false god, the men of the town sought to kill him.

Gideon remained somewhat reluctant – even after these events, but we can learn an important lesson here. Sometimes we are ready to launch out and do something for the Lord, and we may be called by God for the task before us. We should not be surprised, however, when we are in a hurry and God is not. There may be things much closer to home or in our individual lives that God wants us to address first. For Gideon, dealing with the idolatry close to home was a test of obedience. If he was not ready to destroy the family Baal altar, then he was not yet ready to fight the Midianites.

We may recall certain times when we were ready to dive into something and the mission or cause was truly important, but there were obstacles and hindrances for no apparent reason. God knows when we are ready, and He knows when we aren't. As much as we tend to be in a hurry, He isn't. Trust His will, but also trust His timing. Be obedient in what you need to do today.

HEAD TO HEART

- Have you ever been frustrated with God's timing when you are ready to do something and He isn't?

- What are some of the tests that God has placed in your life to prepare and refine you?

- Are there any "small" areas of obedience you have neglected as you look to bigger things that God may do later?

DAY 35

FAITH OR FLEECE?

Then Gideon said to God, "If you will save Israel by my hand, as you have said, behold, I am laying a fleece of wool on the threshing floor. If there is dew on the fleece alone, and it is dry on all the ground, then I shall know that you will save Israel by my hand, as you have said." And it was so. When he rose early next morning and squeezed the fleece, he wrung enough dew from the fleece to fill a bowl with water. Then Gideon said to God, "Let not your anger burn against me; let me speak just once more. Please let me test just once more with the fleece. Please let it be dry on the fleece only, and on all the ground let there be dew." And God did so that night; and it was dry on the fleece only, and on all the ground there was dew.

Judges 6:36-40

Before we are too critical of Gideon and his request for a sign from God, followed by *another* sign from God, we at least can be sympathetic that what God had told Gideon to do wasn't easy. Also, Gideon didn't have the book of Judges, as we do, to see how the story turned out! Most of us can identify with believing that God has spoken something to us but also wanting to be sure before we act. (*Maybe God said that . . . or maybe it was the anchovies I ate the night before.*) However, that really isn't what Gideon was doing with the fleece. This also is not a good way for us to seek to hear from the Lord – we have the Holy Spirit.

Gideon was not trying to make sure he had heard God correctly – he had and he knew it. He said, "If you will save Israel by my hand, as you have said . . . ." Gideon knew what God had said, but he apparently was attempting to guarantee the outcome or perhaps get out of the assignment. He was asking God to "jump through hoops" to ensure he would be successful. If God were going to give him a way out, he would gladly take it.

Gideon's example here is a far cry from walking by faith and trusting in the Holy Spirit's guidance. We don't need to "lay out a fleece," but we do need to train ourselves to be sensitive to His leading and immerse ourselves in the Word of God and prayer because then we will be able to best hear His voice. We probably aren't going to get any guarantees of success or how everything will go. We simply need to obey. Pray and keep praying, but then trust and obey.

HEAD TO HEART

- How has God made known His will to you? How will you seek to know His will in the future?

- Are there any ways in which you are hesitating to obey the Lord or wishing He would make everything more certain?

- Knowing that Gideon was really testing God instead of simply obeying Him, why do you think God still "played along"?

DAY 36

LESS IS MORE

The LORD said to Gideon, "The people with you are too many for me to give the Midianites into their hand, lest Israel boast over me, saying, 'My own hand has saved me.' Now therefore proclaim in the ears of the people, saying, 'Whoever is fearful and trembling, let him return home and hurry away from Mount Gilead.'" Then 22,000 of the people returned, and 10,000 remained. And the LORD said to Gideon, "The people are still too many. Take them down to the water, and I will test them for you there, and anyone of whom I say to you, 'This one shall go with you,' shall go with you, and anyone of whom I say to you, 'This one shall not go with you,' shall not go." ... And the LORD said to Gideon, "With the 300 men who lapped I will save you and give the Midianites into your hand, and let all the others go every man to his home."

Judges 7:2-7

Sometimes less is more or at least less was more with Gideon's army. When you are about to go into battle, "the more the merrier" would seem like a better motto, but it wasn't God's plan. Not only is God all powerful, but He also knows a thing or two about human nature. Gideon started with an army of 32,000 men, which sounds respectable. But the Bible says this about their enemy: "And the Midianites and the Amalekites and all the people of the East lay along the valley like locusts in abundance, and their camels were without number, as the sand that is on the seashore in abundance" (Judges 7:12). Suddenly, 32,000 troops didn't sound nearly as formidable; but God still commanded a dramatic troop reduction from 32,000 to 10,000 to 300. Gideon and his remaining 300 men might have thought to themselves that it made no sense to reduce the number of troops when they were about to face such a strong opponent – the same opponent who had oppressed them the last seven years. But God could have saved them with just one person, so 300 were more than enough.

But why? God knew that, if they won with great numbers, they would take credit for the victory and glorify themselves. It would be as though God had done nothing and as if they won the victory all by themselves. That was the very reason the people of Israel were already in the predicament of Midianite oppression – they had forgotten God. If this sounds cynical, the next chapter in Judges reveals how the success truly went to Gideon's head.

God knew the Israelites and Gideon all too well – just as He knows our tendencies also. Many of us could not handle the success or victory we are seeking. Don't be afraid of a situation that seems impossible. God is not limited to what makes sense to our analysis. God may be doing things the way He is so that no confusion remains as to who should receive the glory.

HEAD TO HEART

- What causes our tendency to make everything about ourselves and seek glory for ourselves?

- Why would God instruct Gideon to eliminate the fearful and trembling first? Wasn't there good reason to be afraid?

- Do you think there was a special significance to how the men drank the water, or was this merely a way to reduce the number to 300?

DAY 37

MAKING IT ABOUT ME

And he divided the 300 men into three companies and put trumpets into the hands of all of them and empty jars, with torches inside the jars. And he said to them, "Look at me, and do likewise. When I come to the outskirts of the camp, do as I do. When I blow the trumpet, I and all who are with me, then blow the trumpets also on every side of all the camp and shout, 'For the LORD and for Gideon.'"

Judges 7:16-18

One of the interesting things about reading the events of the Old Testament is that often the narrator does not comment on the story he is telling – he simply tells the story, leaving us to think about the implications. This is a prime example. As Gideon had narrowed his army to 300 men and equipped them with jars, trumpets and torches, the time had come to face the Midianites. Gideon was acting in obedience to God's commands – although a lot of motivation had been required to get Gideon to this point. But then something happened.

Gideon's instructions were for the men to shout, "For the LORD and for Gideon!" For Gideon? Was this for the Lord *and* for Gideon? Now, if everything else had gone smoothly after the battle and Gideon was able to handle the success of defeating the Midianites, we probably wouldn't think much of Gideon's charge to the army. By itself, we might be able to give Gideon the benefit of the doubt.

The issue is that the post-battle Gideon was a train wreck, and this is our first indication of what would come in the next chapter. Judges 8 reveals that Gideon came to see himself, at best, as a celebrity and, at worst, an equal with God. Why couldn't the shout simply be for the Lord? Why does Gideon, who had been reluctant to obey God through the whole process, now get to share the glory with God?

May we never underestimate our tendencies to make everything about ourselves – even to the point of taking credit for what God has done. We never want to plagiarize God. Pride and selfishness often come in subtle forms. Gideon was once timid and fearful; but when he was given the opportunity to do something great, he began to pursue glory for himself. As the story unfolds, Gideon moves further and further away from any sense of humility or gratitude. So here is the question: Are we willing to serve God faithfully if all the glory goes to Him?

HEAD TO HEART

- Do you think Gideon was revealing an ulterior motive or innocently issuing a rallying cry?

- In what ways have you seen people pat themselves on the back instead of glorifying God?

- How do we deal with the pride in our hearts that craves glory for ourselves?

DAY 38

WEAPONS OF WAR

So Gideon and the hundred men who were with him came to the outskirts of the camp at the beginning of the middle watch, when they had just set the watch. And they blew the trumpets and smashed the jars that were in their hands. Then the three companies blew the trumpets and broke the jars. They held in their left hands the torches, and in their right hands the trumpets to blow. And they cried out, "A sword for the LORD and for Gideon!" Every man stood in his place around the camp, and all the army ran. They cried out and fled. When they blew the 300 trumpets, the LORD set every man's sword against his comrade and against all the army. And the army fled as far as Beth-shittah toward Zererah, as far as the border of Abel-meholah, by Tabbath.

Judges 7:19-22

We make our plans and set our course, but God doesn't necessarily check with us first on how to proceed. In the first place, if we had been assigned the task of selecting the next deliverer/judge for Israel, we probably would not have picked Gideon. But God did.

If we were about to engage in battle with a formidable, numerous enemy, we would not have reduced the number of our troops to only 300 and further split them into three companies. But God did. And although they did not have the most sophisticated weapons in the days of the judges, we probably still would have tried to equip the troops with more than a torch, a jar and a trumpet. But again, that's what God did. But the difference is that God's strategy worked.

Our situations are different, but we have battles to fight as well. We tend to worry, fret, analyze and strategize when God already has secured our success. From a human standpoint, it wasn't the best battle strategy ever devised, but it didn't need to be because God would cause the strange strategy to succeed. The enemy was thrown into confusion because of a simple act of obedience. Blow the trumpets, break the jars and shout.

Now, while it could be entertaining, blowing a trumpet, breaking a jar and shouting will likely not be the best strategy for the battle you are fighting. Still, the simplest things are effective when the battle belongs to the Lord. We see this with Moses (Exodus 14) and again with Jehoshaphat. (2 Chronicles 20) When the battle is overwhelming, remember the battle isn't yours but His. When you start to think you can handle things on your own, stand down and wait for God to go before you.

HEAD TO HEART

- Do you think Gideon's small army felt ridiculous or powerful with their plan of attack?

- Do you tend to spend more time and energy analyzing and strategizing or praying and trusting?

- What kind of impact do you think this victory would have had upon Gideon and his army?

DAY 39

TIME AND TIME AGAIN

For everything there is a season,
and a time for every matter under heaven:
a time to be born, and a time to die;
a time to plant, and a time to pluck up what is planted;
a time to kill, and a time to heal;
a time to break down, and a time to build up;
a time to weep, and a time to laugh;
a time to mourn, and a time to dance;
a time to cast away stones, and a time to gather stones together;
a time to embrace, and a time to refrain from embracing;
a time to seek, and a time to lose;
a time to keep, and a time to cast away;
a time to tear, and a time to sew;
a time to keep silence, and a time to speak;
a time to love, and a time to hate;
a time for war, and a time for peace.

Ecclesiastes 3:1-8

Even people who aren't familiar with Ecclesiastes probably have heard these words in the song "Turn! Turn! Turn!" by the Byrds who helped make these words famous; but these words spoke profound truth long before they were put to music in the 1960s since they are Scripture. The Preacher tells us that life consists of times and seasons for everything. In some seasons we thrive, and in others we struggle. Changes in our lives can be difficult, but we can be thankful that God has blessed us with different seasons. Not every day or every chapter of our lives is the same, and we can appreciate and be thankful for the variety.

With all of the various times and seasons mentioned, the word "and" also is important. You've probably also noticed that every season seems to be a mixture of both joys and trials. Weeping *and* laughing. Mourning *and* dancing. In all the "ands" are opportunities to grow and know Jesus better through them.

If we are in a season of mostly mourning and struggle, we can rejoice because what we are enduring is just for a season, but another season will come eventually. If we mostly are rejoicing, we don't have to despair that a bad season is coming right after. We can be thankful for that season while it lasts. If every season was what we consider to be good, then we wouldn't enjoy any of them. But even in the tough seasons – the times for weeping, mourning and seeking – we can rejoice because, through Jesus, every season is redeemed and every trial is purposeful. When it is time to die, then we get to really live.

HEAD TO HEART

- How would you describe the season in which God has you right now?

- What is He teaching you in this season of your life?

- Have you regretted not enjoying a season of life more than you did? Are you usually looking ahead instead of being present?

HOSEA: COSTLY FORGIVENESS

And the LORD said to me, "Go again, love a woman who is loved by another man and is an adulteress, even as the LORD loves the children of Israel, though they turn to other gods and love cakes of raisins." So I bought her for fifteen shekels of silver and a homer and a lethech of barley. And I said to her, "You must dwell as mine for many days. You shall not play the whore, or belong to another man; so will I also be to you." For the children of Israel shall dwell many days without king or prince, without sacrifice or pillar, without ephod or household gods. Afterward the children of Israel shall return and seek the LORD their God, and David their king, and they shall come in fear to the LORD and to his goodness in the latter days.

Hosea 3:1-5

What is the hardest thing you've ever done? Hosea was asked to do an extraordinarily difficult thing – to say the least. Not only was Hosea commanded to accept back his adulterous wife, but he would have to pay the price to retrieve her. And yet what God was asking Hosea to do was nothing that He would not do Himself – at the cost of His Son. "All we like sheep have gone astray"; but God would pay the price to redeem us, providing the Way to show mercy to us and vindicate His righteousness. (Romans 3:21-26)

Forgiveness is costly. If we hold on to the resentment, the bitterness will cost us spiritually, emotionally and even physically. If we move towards forgiveness, we must somehow absorb the cost of what was done by the offender. Hosea probably didn't fully understand what he was doing and how God's requirement of him pointed to what Jesus would do centuries later. But Hosea could understand enough to know that adultery was the very thing Israel was doing to God and that his role was to proclaim this message. Hosea's life was a painful but powerful picture of God's faithfulness and a foreshadowing of Christ.

On this side of the cross, we see more clearly what God was doing. He not only would forgive our sins but also would pay the price of forgiveness on our behalf. His forgiveness of our sins means that our forgiving others is not optional. The forgiven forgive. Forgiving others always is costly; but considering the price paid by Jesus, any price we pay to forgive is small in comparison. When we are choosing to walk through the process of forgiving someone else, we experience in deeper ways our forgiveness – unmerited and freely given. The journey will not be easy, but we'll be walking in the steps of Jesus and setting ourselves free.

HEAD TO HEART

- Would you be able to forgive adultery? How far would you go to receive the person back?

- Is there anyone that you simply refuse to forgive? Who have you truly forgiven?

- Have you found that forgiveness is more of a single decision or a long process?

DAY 41

JOEL: THE RESTORATION PROJECT

Be glad, O children of Zion, and rejoice in the LORD your God, for he has given the early rain for your vindication; he has poured down for you abundant rain, the early and the latter rain, as before. The threshing floors shall be full of grain; the vats shall overflow with wine and oil. I will restore to you the years that the swarming locust has eaten, the hopper, the destroyer, and the cutter, my great army, which I sent among you. You shall eat in plenty and be satisfied, and praise the name of the LORD your God, who has dealt wondrously with you. And my people shall never again be put to shame. You shall know that I am in the midst of Israel, and that I am the LORD your God and there is none else. And my people shall never again be put to shame.

Joel 2:23-27

The first chapter of Joel describes a plague of devouring locusts that ravaged the land until there was nothing left. These events served as a call to repentance for God's people. Judgment had come and even more was coming, but in that judgment was the opportunity to repent. "'Yet even now,' declares the LORD, 'return to me with all your heart, with fasting, with weeping, and with mourning; and rend your hearts and not your garments.' Return to the LORD your God, for he is gracious and merciful, slow to anger, and abounding in steadfast love; and he relents over disaster" (Joel 2:12-13).

When they repented, God moved in power and restored the land. The land was green and flourishing once again. Repentance brings restoration; but even more than that, God promised to restore the time that the locusts had eaten.

While we may not be expecting a plague of locusts, many of us can look back at seasons of our lives with deep regret over the opportunities we wasted and the wrong things we did. Even though all of the consequences don't necessarily go away in this life, God brings newness and restoration – even after we blow it on a grand scale. God's grace and redemption are much more than just a second chance.

But why would He do that – given that we made our bed? Because when He brings restoration and newness in our lives, they result in praise. We become astonished with His goodness, and we have grateful hearts because He has dealt wonderfully with us. Even more, He takes away the shame we have carried, and we get to be free from the past. He is the Lord our God, and nothing or no one compares to Him. All of our transgression is no match for His mercy. Once and for all, the payment for our sins was settled on the cross. It is *finished*.

HEAD TO HEART

- Do you ever struggle with feelings of guilt over past indiscretions or wasted opportunities?

- What is the difference between true repentance and regret from consequences?

- Even if you have been a Christian for a long time, are you still deeply affected by His grace and forgiveness?

DAY 42

AMOS: WORTHLESS WORSHIP

I hate, I despise your feasts, and I take no delight in your solemn assemblies. Even though you offer me your burnt offerings and grain offerings, I will not accept them; and the peace offerings of your fattened animals, I will not look upon them. Take away from me the noise of your songs; to the melody of your harps I will not listen. But let justice roll down like waters, and righteousness like an ever-flowing stream.

Amos 5:21-24

If we simply read the passage without any context, we might assume we're reading the complaining of a disgruntled churchgoer. But God was speaking, and a sad situation led Him to say these words. The people of Israel were making the offerings and going through the rituals of their religion, but all the things they were doing were just that – religious rituals. Their service to God had no bearing on the rest of their lives. They saw no issue with worshiping God part of the time but having other gods as well. Sadly, this attitude persists to this day. Today we call this religious pluralism. The individual is the center of everything, getting to pick and choose the aspects from each religion that seem most appealing or convenient.

Additionally, God was not being honored in the way His people treated one another. Justice and righteousness were absent from their daily lives. They would claim to be serving Yahweh while cheating and mistreating other people. Yahweh is Lord over everything, but the people were attempting to compartmentalize Him into only certain areas of their lives.

When God spoke through Amos, he was clear that His patience was running out. "Take away from me the noise of your songs" (Amos 5:23). We might wonder if God wouldn't say the same thing in response to some of our worship gatherings today. We put a great deal of emphasis on worship style and keeping up with the latest and greatest worship songs, but does any of that truly reflect how we actually live? On our best day, our worship is imperfect. We sing and say things we don't always mean and inconsistently live these things out. God knows the difference between authenticity and merely going through the motions.

While someday we will be made whole and complete, we aren't there yet, and neither is our worship and service. The comfort is that none of this, of course, comes as a surprise to God. The challenge is to continually seek to make our words and actions match what we say in worship, to live a *lifestyle* of worship.

HEAD TO HEART

- Have you ever felt that a worship service was more offensive than pleasing to God? What made it that way?

- What is the difference(s) between authentic worship from flawed people and hypocritical worship that is a stench to God?

- What role do our emotions play in authentic worship? How do we measure the worth of our worship?

DAY 43

OBADIAH: GOD NOTICED

Behold, I will make you small among the nations; you shall be utterly despised. The pride of your heart has deceived you, you who live in the clefts of the rock, in your lofty dwelling, who say in your heart, "Who will bring me down to the ground?" Though you soar aloft like the eagle, though your nest is set among the stars, from there I will bring you down, declares the LORD. . . . For the day of the LORD is near upon all the nations. As you have done, it shall be done to you; your deeds shall return on your own head.

Obadiah 2-4, 15

Sometimes we hear the phrase that someone is "getting away with murder" when they are doing all of the wrong things without seeming to suffer any consequences. The relatively tiny book of Obadiah was written to assure the Edomites that they were not going to get away with murder or anything else. The Edomites needed to know that God knew.

Who were the Edomites, and why was God out to get them? The people of Edom were the descendants of Esau, who was the brother of Jacob back in Genesis. The people of Israel (later divided into Israel and Judah) were the descendants of Jacob. Since Jacob had been clearly favored over Esau, there was always a rivalry between them and subsequently their descendants, which continued even until the days of Obadiah. Still, the Edomites were relatives of the people of Judah – even if distant relatives by this time.

When God raised up the Babylonians to conquer Jerusalem and the people of Judah, the Edomites rejoiced and celebrated. They offered neither help nor refuge to Judah, celebrating as their relatives were dragged away. Although God had allowed judgment on Judah, He would not allow the Edomites to gloat in their sufferings. The Edomites must not have read Proverbs 24:17, "Do not rejoice when your enemy falls, and let not your heart be glad when he stumbles." Even on a national level, kicking someone when they are down is a bad idea. Obadiah prophesied to let the Edomites know they were about to get what was coming to them.

Now even if we appreciate justice and are pleased when things turn out fairly, why is God's justice on Edom thousands of years ago still significant? Why does it matter that an ancient people got what they deserved? At the very least, we receive the assurance that God will make things right. We are reminded that nothing escapes His notice. Sometimes consequences come in a way that we get to see them happen; but if not, we know that another day of judgment is coming. Today be faithful to the Lord – despite what others may be doing. God always sees. God always knows.

HEAD TO HEART

- Do you see the evil in the world and sometimes wonder if God is ever going to act?

- Since God Himself had brought judgment on Judah, why was it not acceptable for the Edomites to rub it in their faces?

- Have you ever heard a sermon or a Bible study on Obadiah? Why are some books of the Bible so often ignored?

DAY 44

JONAH: CHASED BY GRACE

Then Jonah prayed to the LORD his God from the belly of the fish, saying, "I called out to the LORD, out of my distress, and he answered me; out of the belly of Sheol I cried, and you heard my voice. For you cast me into the deep, into the heart of the seas, and the flood surrounded me; all your waves and your billows passed over me. Then I said, 'I am driven away from your sight; yet I shall again look upon your holy temple.' The waters closed in over me to take my life; the deep surrounded me; weeds were wrapped about my head at the roots of the mountains. I went down to the land whose bars closed upon me forever; yet you brought up my life from the pit, O LORD my God. When my life was fainting away, I remembered the LORD, and my prayer came to you, into your holy temple. Those who pay regard to vain idols forsake their hope of steadfast love. But I with the voice of thanksgiving will sacrifice to you; what I have vowed I will pay. Salvation belongs to the LORD!"

Jonah 2:1-9

One of the amazing things about Jonah's prayer from the belly of the fish was that he prayed *"from the belly of the fish."* Jonah was not out of the situation yet – or was he? Salvation came before Jonah was hurled onto the dry land. God already had rescued him when he was about to go under for the last time. The fish already had been appointed to swallow Jonah alive before he was drowning and before he repented. (1:17)

God certainly could have let Jonah run away completely. Even if there was never a big storm at sea, God could have allowed Jonah to just keep running away and never come back. After all, running away was Jonah's choice. He would have deserved whatever his "free will" brought him. But God pursued Jonah. He refused to let Jonah simply run away if that were even possible. In His grace, God pursued the reluctant prophet.

The storm was by God's design and a sign of His mercy. Even when it meant bringing Jonah to the point of death and despair, God still was reaching out to Jonah. Being swallowed alive by a fish was miraculous – not just because of this rare occurrence but also because the fish's belly became the place where Jonah met with God. Even in the darkness of the great fish's stomach, Jonah knew he had been rescued. He knew that God had been merciful. And what's more, Jonah knew only the true and living God could do that. As he later said so powerfully, "Those who pay regard to vain idols forsake their hope of steadfast love" (Jonah 2:8). Jonah tried to run away, but God's steadfast love chased after him.

The rest of the story demonstrates that Jonah still was something of a mess. Yes, he did go and preach to Nineveh; but much to his chagrin, the Ninevites *repented*. But what really upset Jonah was that he knew that God would show them mercy. (4:1-4) Having dramatically experienced God's grace in his life, Jonah still wanted wrath for his enemies. The book of Jonah ends abruptly with God asking Jonah if He should not have pity on the Ninevites. We are not certain how Jonah answered the question, but we are faced with the same question: Is God's grace only for us or for our enemies as well?

HEAD TO HEART

- With these things in mind, do you think it was fear that motivated Jonah to flee from God's command to go and preach to Nineveh, or was it something else?

- The violent storm and the great fish seem like a lot of trouble. Why didn't God just let Jonah go and send someone else to Nineveh?

- What person or what group of people do you struggle with loving and hoping to see them receive God's grace?

DAY 45

MICAH: WHO IS LIKE YAHWEH?

Who is a God like you, pardoning iniquity and passing over transgression for the remnant of his inheritance? He does not retain his anger forever, because he delights in steadfast love. He will again have compassion on us; he will tread our iniquities underfoot. You will cast all our sins into the depths of the sea. You will show faithfulness to Jacob and steadfast love to Abraham, as you have sworn to our fathers from the days of old.

Micah 7:18–20

The name of the prophet Micah means "Who is like Yahweh?"; so Micah begins this final section of his book with the question raised by his name. Of course, the answer is there is no one like Him, and the verses that follow explain why. Micah is a book detailing God's judgment but also His forgiveness. Having given much attention to the sins of Israel and Judah and the consequences that were headed their way, Micah praises the Lord who also will show compassion.

Not only will He forgive our sins, but He will remove them from us. Why? Because He delights in steadfast love. The promises that He made to Jacob and Abraham concerning their descendants were the same promises He now was keeping – even though the people were undeserving and Jacob and Abraham had long since been dead. Their faithfulness never merited God's compassion and forgiveness – it was based solely on His faithfulness.

If this was true before Jesus came, how much more so now because of His conquering sin and death on the cross? Judgment and wrath were poured out on the only One who was not deserving, and His perfect record of righteousness was credited to us. The enemy loves to throw our sin back in our face, keeping us focused on our sin and failure rather than on what God has done. He does not deal with us according to our sin but according to His faithfulness and according to the righteousness of Jesus. (2 Corinthians 5:21) Truly, who is a God like Him?

HEAD TO HEART

- Do you sometimes struggle with guilt or shame over past sins and failures?

- How was God able to maintain His justice in not passing over our sins but showing us His grace and His mercy – all at the same time?

- Does His forgiveness motivate you towards sinning because it already is forgiven or towards living righteously since you have been declared righteous in Christ?

DAY 46

NAHUM: WHEN GOD THROWS FILTH

Behold, I am against you, declares the LORD of hosts, and will lift up your skirts over your face; and I will make nations look at your nakedness and kingdoms at your shame. I will throw filth at you and treat you with contempt and make you a spectacle. And all who look at you will shrink from you and say, "Wasted is Nineveh; who will grieve for her?" Where shall I seek comforters for you?

Nahum 3:5-7

If that is what the Lord of hosts is saying to you, then you are, we might say, not in a very good place. Good news! God is neither throwing filth at us nor treating us with contempt. These words were not and are not being spoken to us, but they were what God was saying to the Assyrians through the prophet Nahum. With Nahum's name meaning "comfort," the theme of the book is that the people of Judah would be comforted to know that God was bringing judgment on their cruel enemies, the Assyrians.

There was no room for gloating since God had allowed the Assyrians to bring judgment on His people, but the Assyrians did not get away with their cruelty. God can use a nation and still judge a nation because, all the while, that nation presumes to be ruling the world. The Babylonians would make the same assumption after the Assyrians were gone. The Medes and the Persians would do the same after the Babylonians. Nations rise and fall as God remains fully in control.

The language used here is graphic, and it's surprising to picture God throwing filth at people – let alone the utter humiliation of their skirt being lifted over their faces. But in that humiliation of the Assyrians, there was comfort for God's people. The Assyrians were guilty too, and now God was dealing with them. Evil would not go unpunished; no one was getting away with anything.

Something we rarely stop to consider is the punishment for our sins and rebellion against the Lord. Is it fair that we don't get what we deserve? If God just overlooks our rebellion and failure, how can He be holy and righteous? But the amazing thing is that God didn't overlook our sin at all – there was indeed punishment meted out for all of our sins. God would have been perfectly fair to treat each of us as He did the Assyrians. Instead of unleashing His wrath on us, God offered up His Son to bear the punishment for us. There was punishment, and justice was administered. But Jesus took all of that wrath and punishment, so we can receive His mercy and His grace. Nothing can bring more "nahum" than resting in those truths.

HEAD TO HEART

- How could God use Nahum to bring comfort even as judgment was falling on the Assyrians?

- Is there an aspect of God's judgment that is comforting?

- How does the message of the Gospel bring "nahum," which is comfort, to our broken world?

DAY 47

HABAKKUK: ASKING GOD WHY

O LORD, how long shall I cry for help, and you will not hear? Or cry to you "Violence!" and you will not save? Why do you make me see iniquity, and why do you idly look at wrong? Destruction and violence are before me; strife and contention arise. So the law is paralyzed, and justice never goes forth. For the wicked surround the righteous; so justice goes forth perverted.

Habakkuk 1:2-4

No one could accuse Habakkuk of starting out on a light or chipper note. He has questions for God and jumps right into asking them. Many years have passed, but we might notice that we are asking some of those same questions. But even more than asking questions, Habakkuk was making direct statements with the questions he raised with God.

Habakkuk essentially makes three contentions as he prays to Yahweh:

1) You're not *listening*. **"O LORD, how long shall I cry for help, and you will not hear?"** Habakkuk felt what we probably have felt also as we do everything we know to do in a situation, but nothing is working or changing. Maybe you've been told all of your life, "Just pray about it" or "Let go and let God." But you did pray – a lot. You let go and you let God, but He hasn't done squat – at least not yet. In subtle ways, however, our attitude can suggest that God *must* do something because we prayed. While we are right to pour our hearts out to the Lord, we are wrong to see prayer as merely trying to get God to do something. Sometimes God's answer is no. Sometimes He is telling us to wait. When

we're frustrated that God doesn't seem to be listening, maybe we are the ones who aren't listening.

2) You're not *doing anything*. **"Or cry to you "Violence!" and you will not save? Why do you make me see iniquity, and why do you idly look at wrong? Destruction and violence are before me; strife and contention arise."** Does Habakkuk's description of his day remind you of your own? The downside of serving God, who is all powerful and who can do anything, is that there will be things that you think He should be doing; but He isn't doing them. You likely would do certain things if you only had the power to do them, but you don't. We tend to believe these are the things that God *should* be doing because He can! But it doesn't quite work that way, does it? Most of our frustration with God centers around His not doing what we think He should. And that was Habakkuk's complaint as well.

3) You're not *winning*. **"So the law is paralyzed, and justice never goes forth. For the wicked surround the righteous; so justice goes forth perverted."** Habakkuk argued that it's not supposed to be this way. With our limited perspective and understanding, sometimes we have difficulty reconciling what we know to be true about God with what we see in the world. The law, especially God's law, is ignored and justice doesn't happen. The wicked seem to be winning, and the result is the perversion. And it wasn't just "out there." Habakkuk lamented what he was seeing among his own people and why God was allowing the wickedness to continue.

In the rest of the book of Habakkuk, God answered him in powerful ways. Many of the answers were not what Habakkuk anticipated or wanted, but God responded nonetheless. The world has changed drastically since Habakkuk's day; but then again, much has stayed the same. If we are asking God a lot of why questions, we find comfort in knowing that we aren't the first and won't be the last. Even if the answers aren't what we expected or if we later discover that we were asking the wrong questions, we still have every assurance that God hears, God acts and, in the end, God wins.

HEAD TO HEART

- Is it okay to speak to God in the manner that Habakkuk did, asking Him why?

- Are you devoting as much energy to listening to God as you are talking to Him?

- If you asked God those same questions, what do you think He would say and how would He say it?

DAY 48

ZEPHANIAH: THE DAY OF THE LORD

"At that time I will search Jerusalem with lamps, and I will punish the men who are complacent, those who say in their hearts, 'The LORD will not do good, nor will he do ill.' Their goods shall be plundered, and their houses laid waste. Though they build houses, they shall not inhabit them; though they plant vineyards, they shall not drink wine from them." The great day of the LORD is near, near and hastening fast; the sound of the day of the LORD is bitter; the mighty man cries aloud there.

Zephaniah 1:12-14

To assume that the patience of God is somehow a sign of indifference is a bad idea. God does care, and what we do matters to Him. Zephaniah prophesied to the people of Judah to warn them about the coming Day of the Lord, but their attitude was characterized by complacency. They were gambling that God would not act at all – whether it was "good or ill."

Not surprisingly, the mindset that God is merely watching from a distance and is not significantly involved in the events of our lives is still very much around today. People live as if there will be no consequences, no day of reckoning. In the days of Noah, the people wagered that Noah was a fool to build an ark – supposedly at God's command. But they bet on the wrong horse. The people of Israel never believed that God would deal with their spiritual adultery – until He did.

And now the people of Judah foolishly gambled that God would never act. Even though the prophet warned them and there was ample opportunity to repent, most didn't. When God raised up the

Babylonians to conquer and enslave His people, they should not have been surprised. But all of that is in the past. We have all of the previous examples with no excuse but to live our lives in a way that pleases Him. Just as surely as He will bring judgment on those who have ignored and disregarded Him, so He will reward those who have lived for His glory.

The Day of the Lord is coming; but if we still have today, we also have opportunities to help others escape what is coming. One of the many reasons that evil is so present in the world is because hope is so absent. 1 Peter 3:15-16 says, "but in your hearts honor Christ the Lord as holy, always being prepared to make a defense to anyone who asks you for a reason *for the hope that is in you*; yet do it with gentleness and respect, having a good conscience, so that, when you are slandered, those who revile your good behavior in Christ may be put to shame."

Live in such a way that others see that you have hope. Some will resent you; but others will want the hope you have, and it's an opportunity to tell them how – and who.

HEAD TO HEART

- In what ways do you see attitudes of complacency toward God in the world?

- In what ways do you see attitudes of complacency toward God among fellow Christians?

- In what ways do you see attitudes of complacency toward God in your life? Which of the three questions was easiest to answer?

DAY 49

HAGGAI: PUTTING ME FIRST

Thus says the LORD of hosts: "These people say the time has not yet come to rebuild the house of the LORD." Then the word of the LORD came by the hand of Haggai the prophet, "Is it a time for you yourselves to dwell in your paneled houses, while this house lies in ruins? Now, therefore, thus says the LORD of hosts: 'Consider your ways. You have sown much, and harvested little. You eat, but you never have enough; you drink, but you never have your fill. You clothe yourselves, but no one is warm. And he who earns wages does so to put them into a bag with holes.'"

Haggai 1:2-6

One of the things we see right away from the relatively unknown book of Haggai is that misplaced priorities are not a new development. Haggai prophesied after the return of the exiles to Judah. Although the previous generations had been carried off into slavery and the city of Jerusalem and its temple destroyed, God had fulfilled His promise to restore them to their land. What stood before the people was a long rebuilding process; but soon after the work began, the priorities of the people shifted from the work of the Lord to making themselves comfortable.

Evidently, the people were unable to find the time for the rebuilding of the house of the Lord; but they had found the time to build themselves nice homes. There was nothing wrong with their building nice homes, but the homes took time to build – just like the temple. Apparently, all of their time and energy were only going in one direction. The presence of excess in their homes – combined with the temple still lying in ruins

– reveals what truly was important to them. The word from the Lord to them was to consider their ways. If nothing seemed to be working right, the reason behind the futility was their own disordered priorities.

The lesson from Haggai is not about giving or church buildings but rather a consideration of the things that are most important in our lives. Does our lifestyle reveal that God truly is our highest priority? Or are we, like the people of Judah, living primarily for ourselves? Are we more concerned about our comfort, our security and our satisfaction than being about what God wants us to be doing?

HEAD TO HEART

- What are the highest priorities in your life as revealed by how you spend your time and energy?

- How do we keep the things that are important but not ultimate from taking all of our time?

- How do you strike the balance between taking care of yourself and your family while being devoted to the things of God?

DAY 50

ZECHARIAH: WHEN THE ENEMY ACCUSES

Then he showed me Joshua the high priest standing before the angel of the LORD, and Satan standing at his right hand to accuse him. And the LORD said to Satan, "The LORD rebuke you, O Satan! The LORD who has chosen Jerusalem rebuke you! Is not this a brand plucked from the fire?" Now Joshua was standing before the angel, clothed with filthy garments. And the angel said to those who were standing before him, "Remove the filthy garments from him." And to him he said, "Behold, I have taken your iniquity away from you, and I will clothe you with pure vestments." And I said, "Let them put a clean turban on his head." So they put a clean turban on his head and clothed him with garments. And the angel of the LORD was standing by.

Zechariah 3:1-5

In the vision that the Lord revealed to Zechariah, the high priest Joshua, who is representative of God's people, was being accused by Satan. While bringing accusations is one of the things that the enemy does best, he had grounds for accusation in that Joshua's garments were filthy with excrement. He was defiled and unholy, the picture of filth. He was not fit to stand before the King, and the enemy was taking full advantage of the opportunity. That's what he does even now.

And yet it was the Lord who rebuked Satan. When the high priest had no grounds to respond to the enemy, the Lord responded to the accusations for him. He rebuked Satan and redeemed Joshua. Not only was the Lord not willing to hear Satan's accusations, He removed the grounds for any accusations by clothing Joshua in "pure vestments" and taking away his iniquity. The clean clothes were an outward symbol of the cleansing God had done on the inside. Joshua was clean through and through.

Many of us know the voice of accusation that the enemy brings. Sometimes his accusations are false and baseless, but sometimes we do soil ourselves with sin. Praise the Lord that He does not listen to the accusations of the enemy but has told us that there is now no condemnation for those who are in Christ Jesus. (Romans 8:1) He also tells us that the written record that stood against us was nailed to the cross with Jesus. (Colossians 2:13-14) Yes, the Holy Spirit convicts us of our sins and moves us to confess them; but the enemy seeks to make us feel condemned and far away from the Lord. Since Satan feeds us lies and accusations, we must be filling our hearts and minds continually with the truth of God's Word.

HEAD TO HEART

- What accusations does the enemy bring against you?

- What accusations does the enemy bring against God when you are being tempted?

- What does the confession of our sin accomplish, considering the reality that all of our sins are forgiven in Christ?

DAY 51

MALACHI: DON'T BRING LEFTOVERS

For from the rising of the sun to its setting my name will be great among the nations, and in every place incense will be offered to my name, and a pure offering. For my name will be great among the nations, says the LORD of hosts. But you profane it when you say that the Lord's table is polluted, and its fruit, that is, its food may be despised. But you say, 'What a weariness this is,' and you snort at it, says the LORD of hosts. You bring what has been taken by violence or is lame or sick, and this you bring as your offering! Shall I accept that from your hand? says the LORD. Cursed be the cheat who has a male in his flock, and vows it, and yet sacrifices to the Lord what is blemished. For I am a great King, says the LORD of hosts, and my name will be feared among the nations.

Malachi 1:11-14

As New Testament believers, we can be thankful that Jesus made the ultimate sacrifice for our sins – once and for all – so that a sacrificial system is no longer needed. In Malachi's day, however, many were bringing imperfect sacrifices, animals and other offerings that were defective and clearly not the best that the worshiper had to offer. We easily can dismiss the importance of this since their error is so egregious and because the need to sacrifice no longer remains. Nevertheless, the principle remains and is instructive for us even now.

While the Old Testament sacrificial system – as they knew it – is now obsolete, the question remains as to whether or not we are giving God our best. The reality that Jesus paid it all does not mean we now can offer to God the scraps of our lives. All too often we give Him what is left of our time, what is left of our money, what is left of our energy – once we have done the things that are more important to us. We laugh about "re-gifting" presents; but does that, in some way, reflect how we serve God? Many never would think of bringing a half-eaten casserole to the potluck dinner, but they think nothing of giving God our reheated leftovers.

Thankfully, we don't sacrifice animals on the altar; but our "reasonable service" is to offer ourselves (our all) to Him as living sacrifices. Romans 12:1-2 says, "I appeal to you therefore, brothers, by the mercies of God, to present your bodies as a living sacrifice, holy and acceptable to God, which is your spiritual worship (*or reasonable service*). Do not be conformed to this world, but be transformed by the renewal of your mind, that by testing you may discern what is the will of God, what is good and acceptable and perfect." Offering our very selves is giving Him our best and giving Him our all. In the light of His mercies, how can we do any less?

HEAD TO HEART

- Why do you think people offer God less than their best?

- Knowing that God needs nothing from any of us, what is it that He wants from us?

- Are you living your life as an offering to God or using God as an accessory for a life you see as your own?

ALSO FROM THE OLD TESTAMENT DEVOTIONAL SERIES

WALKING IN THE WAY:
A Devotional Journey Through the Scriptures Jesus Read

FEET OF CLAY:
Failures from Yesterday, New Mercies for Today

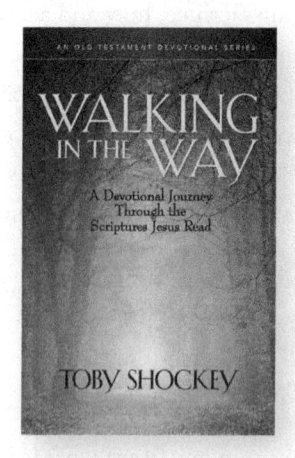

Available on Amazon and other retailers
or directly from the author:

www.mountaintime.org
orders@mountaintime.org

Made in the USA
Columbia, SC
22 March 2025